# THE WAY OF HARMONY

*Also by Jim Dreaver*

THE ULTIMATE CURE
THE HEALING ENERGY WITHIN YOU

SOMATIC TECHNIQUE
A SIMPLIFIED METHOD OF RELEASING CHRONICALLY TIGHT
MUSCLES AND ENHANCING MIND/BODY AWARENESS

# THE WAY OF HARMONY

walking the inner path
to balance, happiness
and success

JIM DREAVER

AVON BOOKS ◆ NEW YORK

Excerpt from "Poem #19" from *The Kabir Book* by Robert Bly. Copyright © 1971, 1977 by Robert Bly. Reprinted by permission of Beacon Press, Boston.

AVON BOOKS, INC.
1350 Avenue of the Americas
New York, New York 10019

Copyright © 1999 by Dr. Jim Dreaver
Cover illustration by Helen D'Souza
Inside back cover author photograph by Jeremy Taunton
Interior design by Kellan Peck
Published by arrangement with the author
ISBN: 0-380-80313-5
**www.avonbooks.com**

Library of Congress Cataloging in Publication Data:

Dreaver, Jim.
    The way of harmony: walking the inner path to balance, happiness, and success / Jim Dreaver.
        p.   cm.
    1. Peace of mind—Religious aspects.   2. Self-realization.   3. Harmony (Philosophy)
4. Success.   5. Happiness.   I. Title.
BL627.55.P4D74   1999                                                99-29548
291.4'4—dc21                                                              CIP

First Avon Books Trade Paperback Printing: October 1999

AVON TRADEMARK REG. U.S. PAT. OFF. AND IN OTHER COUNTRIES, MARCA REGISTRADA, HECHO EN U.S.A.

Printed in the U.S.A.

OPM   10   9   8   7   6   5   4   3   2   1

*For Larry Elsener—*
*Friend, teacher of balance, prince among men.*

# Author's Note

Wherever personal anecdotes are used to illustrate the material in this book, please note that the people involved are aware that their stories are being told. In some cases, names have been changed to protect privacy.

# Contents

# Introduction

*L*et me begin by telling you a true story about my son, Adam, which happened not long after his thirteenth birthday. School was out, and he stayed the night at my house. When I left for my office in the morning, he was still sleeping. Around eleven-thirty, I decided to call and check in on him.

"How's it going, buddy?" I asked. I was a little concerned that he might be wandering around the house, fretting because he had nothing to do.

"Great, Dad," he said. "I just spent an hour reading *Sidhartha,* and then I meditated for twenty minutes."

I smiled and breathed a sigh of relief. I'd bought him Herman Hesse's classic novel about the life of the Buddha a month or two earlier. *Little Buddha* was one of his favorite films. Adam related to the Buddha and his teachings on enlightenment and inner peace.

When I went home at lunchtime I asked him how his meditation went. "It's easy for me now," he said. "I just sit and get really still, and then listen to the sounds around me, like you taught me. That brings me into the present, and my mind gets totally quiet and clear."

Suddenly, his eyes widened as he looked at me. "And Dad . . . !"

"What?" I said, intrigued.

"I could feel the *wholeness* of everything! It gave me a warm, fuzzy feeling inside."

"Wow," I smiled, "that's really cool." It made me happy to realize that he knew how to find that place of wholeness, of spiritual richness, within himself.

"It's important to remember this experience," I said. "Whenever the world out there gets too intense or crazy, you know what to do now to feel really clear and strong inside yourself. You just have to sit like you did, breathe down into your belly, listen to the sounds, and tune in to the power of the present. Then you just let the power flow through you, until you feel all filled up again." I rubbed the back of his head affectionately. "Pretty simple, huh? And pretty awesome, too."

"Yeah, thanks, Dad," he said, and gave me a warm hug. Then we went on to make lunch and talk about what we were going to do for fun that weekend.

Adam's experience with meditation really sums up the message of this book. It is about the inner path to balance, happiness, and success in life. As you learn to make your spiritual well-being your foremost priority, and master the art of getting relaxed, centered, and grounded within, you'll be able to move out into the world—into your relationships, your work, your creative endeavors—with confidence and ease. This is the way of harmony.

If something happens (as it periodically will, for such is the nature of life) to cause frustration, disappointment, pain—or even that learning opportunity we call "failure"—you'll know how to deal with it. This book will give you the information and the tools you need to clear away any conflict or confusion in your mind, harmonize the energy in your body, and tap into the joy that is your true nature. You'll be able to meet life again with a renewed sense of clarity, enthusiasm, passion, and commitment.

You'll feel the inner wholeness that Adam felt. You'll experience a sense of true, inner abundance, a richness of spirit that will always be with you, no matter what is happening outwardly in your life. You'll no longer feel any sense of split between who you are and what you do, between your inner self and your outer world.

The split, the schism between the inner and outer, between the spiritual and material, is probably as old as humanity itself. At a personal level it translates into a conflict between trying to fulfill one's deep spiritual needs and doing what's necessary to prosper in the world.

Many people get caught in one polarity or the other. Some become very spiritual, giving their whole lives over to the pursuit of truth; meanwhile they struggle to pay the rent and make ends meet financially. That was the path I took for many years, and it was my own need for balance, as well as my desire to share the treasure I found—the *core insight*—that inspired this book.

Others go in the opposite direction. The spiritual dimension in life sounds too abstract to them, too idealistic, and so they place all their trust in the material, in the world of the marketplace, money, technology, and things. While they may accumulate material security and do well in the world, there is a chronic dissatisfaction, a lack of real inner peace and happiness, in their heart and soul.

The way to successfully integrate the spiritual and material is by seeing that they are in fact not different from each other but are reflections of the one reality, the one divine consciousness, or energy, that underlies all creation. The more clearly you see this, the easier it is to walk in the world with balance.

This is where the core insight comes in. The core insight, which has its roots in a number of enlightenment teachings of both the East and the West, is the fundamental perspective behind the inner path. It is the knowledge that heals personal conflict, liberates you from fear and limitation, and allows you to fulfill your unique potential—to bloom as the beautiful, conscious, and creative person you really are.

Every person I have ever met who has found genuine inner peace and freedom (and more and more of us are coming into this), has arrived at this understanding, this jewel of wisdom that I call the core insight. This is true whether they discovered it through a formal spiritual practice, contact with an awakened teacher or person, or through their own inquiry and investigation.

The beauty of the core insight is that there is just this one thing, this one idea, that you have to grasp and make real. Not twelve principles, not ten laws, not seven keys, and definitely not a long and arduous journey toward some hoped-for goal of fulfillment, peace, and happiness.

The core insight opens you up to the realization that the happiness you've sought all your life is available right here, right now. You don't have to drop out and go to a monastery or ashram to find it. You can experience it whether you're driving on the freeway, riding the subway, raising a family, working for a corporation, starting a new business, balancing your checkbook, acting on behalf of the environment or social justice, or doing anything else that we humans do. It's your true nature, in fact, and once you awaken to it, it's *always* there—regardless of what may be happening in your outer circumstances.

So, what is it?

The core insight involves a subtle shift in the way you see yourself and your life. It is a stepping back, so to speak, and beginning to see that you are *not* the person you thought you were.

Specifically, you are not your "story." The reality you've created inside your head about who you are—your beliefs, personal history, attitudes, identity, and self-image—is not who you are. This internal reality is actually nothing more than a tale you've been telling yourself, probably for most of your life. It's a fiction, a myth, created out of memory and belief, reinforced through the opinions and judgments of others, and clung to mainly through ignorance and habit.

Before you wake up to your inner, spiritual nature, you need a story, a personal myth, to make sense of the world and your life. We all do. Unfortunately, it's this attachment to the story, to a particular system of belief or way of seeing the world, that explains why there is so much conflict between individuals, cultures, and nations.

People get so identified with their particular version of reality that they will fight, kill, even die for it. It's a sad state of affairs, and it's why we need to continue to raise the level of spiritual awareness on our planet. The freer we all get inwardly, the easier it will be for us to live in peace and harmony with each other so that we can work together to solve the problems facing us.

Enlightenment, then, is seeing that the world you've created inside your head doesn't really exist, except as a fabrication in your mind. You can't actually find a thought anywhere.

The more you see this (and the seeing has to happen over and over again, until your internal "eye"—your true *I*—is fully open), the more the content of your particular story, the baggage from the past, begins to dissolve and drop away. Your head clears, and you feel extraordinarily awake, alive, *present*. Freed of all the psychological and emotional overlay, thinking becomes much more functional—sharper, more intuitive, more creative.

You still have a story, but you're just not identified with it or attached to it anymore. You know it's not who you really are. Your meaning and identity in life come from something much deeper, something much more timeless within you—from the flow and fullness of *being* itself, the energy and power of the life force as it moves through you.

The more you open up to this energy, the more you will experience it as a constantly renewing and revitalizing presence in your life, one that manifests in your body as well-being, in your mind as clarity, and in your heart as love.

Gradually, your ego, your personal sense of "I" and "me," becomes more transparent. All sense of psychological and emotional fear begins to leave you. The world no longer has any real power over you. The big questions—about God, death, the afterlife—resolve themselves in ways you cannot begin to comprehend as long as you're still identified with your story, as long as you still "think" you are the sum of your past, your thoughts, your beliefs.

In this new freedom you find that you no longer need to hold on to any concept or image of "self" to know who you are, or to be happy. Just to *be,* to be alive, aware, and fully engaged in life, is an astonishing enough gift, bringing a depth of meaning and understanding that is beyond words.

Living itself becomes much more spontaneous, creative, playful. You bring a new honesty and energy to your relationships. Your work, the contribution you're here to make, becomes clear. You stop worrying about money. You no longer take problems, difficulties, and other people's judgments personally, because you've stopped taking yourself personally. Imagine how freeing that is!

Most problems, you find, sort themselves out, and those that persist you learn to live with and manage in an intelligent way. Manifestation—the art of translating your inner vision into reality—happens more easily. It's amazing what you can accomplish when you know what you want and your energy is focused on the task before you rather than being attached to the outcome.

Each chapter in this book contains three tools. These are specific exercises that will enable you to better understand and integrate the material being presented. The tools work. Combined with the insights and examples I share, they offer a road map for self-realization. They give you the exact directions you need to come to your *own* experience, your own understanding, of the core insight that is the key to the inner path.

Experiment with the tools. Test them out for yourself. Play with them. Focus on the ones that really make a difference for you. In time, you won't even have to think about when, where, or how to use them. They will become second nature, and their benefits will be deep and lasting.

As you read these pages, it may be helpful to keep in mind that even though inner freedom, once you've found it, is yours forever, attaining balance in the world is very much a *process*.

Because you're human, there will be times—usually when you're under stress, are feeling out of sorts, or are facing a crisis—when the old ego patterns and reactions will tend to resurface and you'll find yourself getting hooked back in by circumstances. The world, and other people, will always try to pull you back into the "story," the drama, and make you forget who and what you really are.

But the deeper your enlightenment, the less you'll be seduced by outer appearances. You'll understand that life is inherently chaotic and uncertain. It is a continual movement, an endless series of events, and conditions are always shifting and changing. Just as the skilled tightrope walker must be supremely alert so as not to fall off the wire when the wind blows, you'll realize that you must be constantly vigilant. You must be ready at a moment's notice to refocus your attention, take a different action, or respond in some other ingenious way to a new or challenging situation.

Balance is a beautiful dance. It feels the best, and it is what works best—for all of us. Whenever your life feels like it's beginning to spin out of control, remember to pause, breathe deeply, come down out of your head, and feel yourself in your body, feel your feet firmly on the earth beneath you. Open your heart and tune in to the sounds around you. Listen for the silence behind the sounds. Feel the energy that is always here, underneath all the noise and chatter inside your head. Feel the energy that you are made of. Feel the power of the present.

Then, from that clear and grounded place, think about the goals and dreams that matter to you, that stir your soul and ignite your passion. These are the ones that are true for you. These are the ones that have the ring of destiny about them.

Focus on the vision you have for your life, the way you see yourself loving and serving. Be true to your heart, and the rest will follow. You'll be fed by an inner joy and zest for life that will always be with you, no matter how difficult your outer circumstances may appear at times. You'll be guided from within. Doors will open, the right people and opportunities will appear. You'll find the strength you need to act. Success will come. Increasingly, gratitude will be your daily prayer.

You'll discover just how incredibly abundant the universe is, once you get in harmony with it.

CHAPTER ONE

# Getting Relaxed in Your Body

## THE SECRET OF RELEASING STRESS

*I*n over twenty years of doing transformational work, I have found that the single most powerful technique for releasing stress and tension in the body and coming to true inner clarity is learning to make your body, senses, and mind *objects* of observation.

In moments of quiet meditation or contemplation, practice looking at your body, its sensations and feelings, as well as the thoughts and images passing through your mind, as you would look at any other object—a tree, a cloud, a car.

It's a process of learning to become a dispassionate observer of your body, mind, and senses. Doing this helps free you from identification with them. Instead of being caught up in your body and mind, and looking out at the world from a place of relative conflict and contraction, pull your awareness back a little, to a place slightly behind and above your head. From there, begin to experience yourself as the *space* in which your body appears, in which breathing happens, in which sensations, feelings, and thoughts arise.

I call this way of observing, or experiencing your own body, mind, and senses, "expanding awareness," and I will describe the actual technique for it a little later in this chapter.

I learned this approach from my spiritual mentor, Jean Klein, a former physician from Europe and a master of Advaita Vedanta, a philosophy that can be thought of as a kind of inner yoga. Advaita, which traces its roots three thousand years back to the Upanishads, the great wisdom scriptures of India, is a way of shifting perception and coming back to the awareness that precedes thinking. It is a direct path to the clear, spacious mind that is our true nature, which gives rise to all that we see, feel, and experience.

When I met Jean after reading his book *The Ease of Being,* I was struck by his presence and the clarity with which he was able to articulate his understanding. He radiated an immense amount of light and love and, like the best teachers, did not take himself for a "teacher," for anyone special. You never felt any sense of ego or personal agenda when you were with him. His focus was solely on pointing us back to the truth, to the teacher within. His influence on me was, literally, life-transforming.

It was Jean who guided me to the core insight—or, as he called it, the "ultimate understanding," the realization that there is actually no "person" who needs to be enlightened, that freedom and happiness are our true nature.

"See through the unreality of self-images and self-concepts, and just be the beautiful person you are," he said. "Then you'll be free."

He himself passed away, at the age of eighty-six, while I was working on this book, but his legacy, and that of his teachers before him, lives on in his written works, in his many students throughout the world, and in these pages.

Health, then, is your natural state, and your body's energies are always seeking their own organic harmony, or wholeness. When you are able to detach yourself from the areas of stress, tension, and pain in your body and just be aware of them without the interference of your analytical mind, they have room to unwind and release. This is not to deny or ignore pain; it is to be present with it in a relaxed, open, non-judging way.

From this neutral place you can feel the length and breadth of your body within your awareness, your consciousness. You can observe the rising and falling of your breath. You can notice the space *around* your body. You can watch the movement of your arms, your legs, your head, your trunk within your visual and sensory field.

The more real this quality of awareness becomes for you, the more you find yourself in the expanded state of consciousness—the sense of ease, of flow, of well-being—that is your true nature. You feel very grounded in and connected to your body. All your senses are alert. You feel awake, clear, extraordinarily present. And behind it all is this tremendous feeling of spaciousness, of freedom.

Gradually, you begin to realize that you don't live in your body, as you had always believed, but your body lives in *you*. This is when you start to really "get" the core insight. It dawns on you that your true nature is pure consciousness, awareness, manifesting in this unique constellation of energy and matter that is your body/mind/self.

To see this is extremely liberating. It frees you from inner conflict and fear, including the fear of failure and even the fear of death, which means you can walk in the world with a much greater feeling of confidence. The information in this chapter is designed to help you embody this concept.

## DEVELOPING A RELATIONSHIP WITH YOUR BODY

Your body is the vehicle for your spirit, the being you really are. Who you are is reflected in your body, in your muscles and joints, the way you breathe, sit, move.

To extend the vehicle analogy, imagine that you are taking a long trip in your car, but your car is a poorly serviced, unreliable clunker that is always breaking down. The trip wouldn't be much fun, would it? It's hard to enjoy the journey when you're constantly worried that your vehicle might not make it. That's why it's important to put energy into taking care of your body—so you can feel good moving around in it.

When you don't feel good in your body—when you are tired, out-of-sorts, when your energy is contracted or stuck—it affects your attitude and makes you think all kinds of negative thoughts. On the other hand, when you have a sensitive and healthy relationship with your body, your attitude always improves.

You know what you need to do. You need to eat right, exercise, and learn how to relax. The good news is that improving your physical well-being doesn't require a major change in your habits and actions. It's really more about a change in *consciousness*—the shifting of attention, or awareness, described above.

In learning to let go of the tension, worry, and stress inside you, you'll start to feel a whole lot better physically, and you'll have more energy. It is psychological and emotional stress that's the real killer—much more so than eating the occasional fatty meal or not exercising for a week or two.

You'll also be much less worried about or afraid of what is happening in your body. People fear unusual sensations or sudden changes in their bodily experience because they don't have a relationship with their bodies. I remember saying to a client once, "Bill, if you had a relationship with your wife like you have with your body, you'd be heading toward a divorce by now." Don't get so divorced from your body that a doctor or therapist has to say that to you!

The best way to help your body do its job of keeping itself in balance is to develop a good relationship with it. That means to stop ignoring it, stop judging it, and start treating it with kindness, affection, and love—just as you would a person you really cared about.

Trust in any relationship needs a certain level of intimacy. Trust itself leads to deeper intimacy. To become intimate with yourself, begin with your body. Start paying attention to the sensations and feelings in your body, to the movement of *energy*.

There's a saying in healing and bodywork circles: energy flows where attention goes. To generate new energy in some area of your life, just give that area more attention. If you want to liven up your marriage or relationship, give it more attention. If you want your work to be more successful, give that more attention. If you've planted a garden and want it to flourish, water it, weed it, and care for it with love—then watch it grow. It's so simple!

To bring new energy into some part of your body, just expand your awareness of that area. To release shoulder tension, for example, bring your awareness into your shoulders and then consciously tighten them by hunching them all the way up around your ears. Breathe in as you do this. Then slowly release your shoulders, breathing out as you do so. Repeat this process several more times, loosely bounce your shoulders up and down, and notice how much more energy you feel in them.

This technique works because by intensifying the problem—the contraction—you're bringing it more into awareness, and that gives you more control over the muscles. It's a law of the body: heightened sensory awareness automatically brings about greater motor control.

You can apply this principle to any tight muscle in your body. Just fully, consciously contract the selected muscle, and then slowly release it. Notice the gradual flood of new sensation and feeling.

## RELAX AND LET GO

Knowing how to relax, to really let go, is the key to being fully at ease in your body. One of the best ways of relaxing is to make *breathing* a conscious exercise. Slow it down to about half its normal rate, and pause briefly between the in-breath and the out-breath. As your breathing slows down, it will become more effortless. Your whole metabolism will begin to calm down. Your pulse rate will drop, and your blood pressure will lower.

The body and mind are not separate. Uncomfortable body sensations cause the mind to worry and fret. Mental conflict, in turn, leads to emotional upset and creates stress in the body. When you learn how to relax your body, your mind will become quieter. There will be less chatter, less mental noise. You'll start to tap into a deeper stillness and clarity. You'll feel a natural balance within.

Practice relaxed breathing, then just be aware of the ever-changing sensations and feelings in your body. Try not to think about them. Just notice them. It will get easier and easier to do this, especially when you apply the tools I'm about to share with you. They will help you create more space inside your own consciousness. As a result, you'll feel more spacious and it will be much easier for you to deal with conflict and upsetting situations.

When people don't like what's happening in their experience, whether it's a condition in their body or a situation in their life, they usually go into immediate resistance and rejection, if not downright denial. If you're honest with yourself, you'll acknowledge that you're probably familiar with this pattern.

But before you can change anything, you first have to accept it, to own it. When you're no longer fighting what's happening, you allow space for the seemingly stuck or uncomfortable energy to unwind and transform.

You can practice this art of transformation through acceptance by beginning with your body. Learn to be a little detached from what you're experiencing in your body. This will give you some freedom from the experience. You won't be so caught up in it, and it will be easier for you to deal with whatever is happening.

It's a welcoming of your experience. You're giving the situation or condition space to *be*. Then the knot of sensation that you have previously labelled "pain" or "tension" can loosen. A new awareness will emerge.

To be aware of your body in this very sensitive, loving way is the most important step you can take in healing yourself physically. Learn to make pain your friend. Soften around it. Give it space to unwind. Even if the pain doesn't go away, the stress around it will lessen. It will become more manageable, more tolerable. Soften your belly, too. Notice how much tension gets held there. Let your belly relax, and your whole being will breathe a sigh of relief.

In the light of clear, present awareness, where there is a calm acceptance of what's happening—rather than denial or resistance—consciousness expands. New insights enter your awareness, the problems at hand reveal their own solutions, and things find their natural stability.

## GET CENTERED AND GROUNDED

Men often die younger than women because they become too hard, especially in their hearts. No wonder there are so many heart attacks and bypass operations. As one surgeon said, the problem is that men have bypassed the heart.

Learning to open your heart comes with deep self-understanding and the willingness to be vulnerable, to trust your feelings and emotions. Openness begins with deepening and slowing the breath, then releasing the tension in your belly, your shoulders, your jaw. This is the first step in getting centered and grounded.

Just as the quickest way to relax a tight muscle is to contract it even further, it's easier to exhale completely if you take a deep inhalation first. You can't truly let go of something until you first acknowledge you *have* it. That's why it's best to intensify the holding of the breath or the muscle before trying to release it.

In learning to center yourself, the trick is to be like the bamboo—firmly rooted in the earth but able to bend and sway with life's forces. Then crisis and change, while they may throw you off a little bit, will always be manageable.

We've already looked at the importance of conscious breathing. Most people's breathing is too fast and too shallow. It's all in their chest. Breath is energy, which means their energy is stuck in the upper part of their body. This makes them unbalanced. They're easily knocked off-center by negative encounters.

You can make centering and grounding an exercise, a somatic/spiritual practice to be used throughout the day, whenever you need it. It provides a firm foundation for the Expanding Awareness technique (Tool #2).

## TOOL #1
### CENTERING AND GROUNDING

It's good to do this exercise standing. Feel your feet firmly on the ground, and unlock your knees. Direct your breath down into your belly, into the place the Japanese call the *hara*, the vital center two inches below your navel. Breathing from here as you consciously connect with the earth beneath you helps you feel strong, centered, grounded. You feel, at a physical level, as if you are being supported by the planet itself. This is tremendously empowering.

Now experiment with sending energy down through your lower body, through your legs, the soles of your feet, into the earth. Visualize the energy in the form of "grounding cords" sinking deep into the earth, giving you a firm foundation, a solid stance.

Then consciously breathe out by pulling your belly in, which forces the diaphragm up and pushes all the air out of your lungs. Exhale slowly. Pause a moment, lock and unlock your knees a few times, then let your belly relax and expand outward. This will automatically bring air into your lungs. Allow the rib cage to expand as you take in even more air. Then let the shoulders rise. Pause another moment.

Repeat this exhalation/inhalation cycle several more times, taking care to balance a long exhalation with a long inhalation. Balancing your in- and out-breath in this way helps your whole metabolism come into balance. Then just relax and be still. Visually connect with your environment. Enjoy the feeling of being alert, centered, present.

It's unrealistic to expect to be centered every waking moment of the day. But when you know your center, the ground you stand on, you come back quickly when some crisis or challenge comes along and knocks you off-center. Sometimes it takes just a few minutes.

## YOU ARE BIGGER THAN YOUR BODY, MIND, AND SENSES

People who are at peace with themselves, who live in a state of dynamic balance, have found a comfortable relationship with their bodies. They may still have pain or sickness, an incurable disease even, but they are not dominated by it. They are connected to something bigger than themselves, and this gives them perspective and freedom.

Centering and Grounding (Tool #1) teaches you to be fully *in* your body, to be fully *embodied*. Tool #2, Expanding Awareness, will help you get free of over-identification with your body, of any feeling you might have of being trapped in your body, or being a victim of it.

As you develop a more conscious relationship with your body, you'll discover that there's a fine line between being *in* your body in a very grounded way and, at the same time, feeling very free in your relationship with it, so that it no longer drags you down, or in some other way inhibits the healing and nourishing flow of energy from moving through you.

The essential message here is that you have a body, but it's not who you are. Healing is about making a perceptual shift. It is understanding—actually seeing—that you are neither your body, mind, or senses. Rather, you are that which is aware of these constantly changing phenomena.

Practice being the space around your body, the space in which your body appears, in which sensations and feelings exist. This will help you develop the ability to simply witness the constantly changing phenomena in your body without getting worried or upset by them. The following meditation will make this real. This is the main technique for opening up to the experience of your true expanded nature—the "secret" I spoke of at the beginning of this chapter.

## TOOL #2
## EXPANDING AWARENESS

Sit comfortably and close your eyes. Bring your awareness to a place slightly behind and above your head (as if "you" are sitting slightly behind and above yourself).

Now, let your awareness expand. Visualize yourself as being pure, expanded awareness—as the clear space in which your body exists. Inwardly see the length and breadth of your body, its shape, its form, within the context of this space. Let your awareness be one with the space.

Begin watching your breath in the same way. Dispassionately observe the rising and falling of your breath. Notice how, as you slow your breathing down, you feel more relaxed. Be aware of the breath coming in and going out, all within the space, the field, of your awareness. Now turn your attention to your mind, your thoughts. Notice how thinking arises from a point behind your eyes. Just watch the thoughts and images arising within your awareness. Let them come and go, like birds flying across the sky. Don't chase after them. Don't get caught up in them. Just be aware of them. Be aware of awareness itself. Be the sky. Let your mind be like the clear, vast sky.

Begin to realize, to accept that awareness—this clarity and vastness—is your true nature. You are the unchanging presence behind all the sensations and feelings in your body, and the thoughts and images passing through your mind. Begin to accept that rather than being a "someone" living inside your body, you *are* this presence, this awareness itself—and your body is an extension of the awareness that you are. Get the sense of yourself as being pure awareness, timeless presence, and your body as being the physical expression, or manifestation, of the awareness that you are.

Pause periodically throughout the day to expand your awareness in this way, so that you can let go of the identification with the *expressions* of awareness—your body, mind, and senses—and open up to who and what you really are.

---

The Expanding Awareness technique will enable you to gradually loosen any unhealthy, obsessive identification you may have with your body. You'll have a lighter, freer, more trusting relationship with it. As you stop fighting and resisting what's happening in your bodily experience, your body's energy naturally finds its own harmony. It's a process of learning to be in the place of detached, yet ever-present, awareness.

If you work with this tool every day (I suggest beginning your morning meditation with it), then in time it will become second nature. Whenever you start to feel stressed, confused, or uptight, you'll find yourself remembering to stop, breathe, and expand your awareness just like I've shown you.

When you are able to breathe easily and simply be present in the moment, you won't be bothered by pain, discomfort, or problems—or, if you are, they won't be such a big deal. You'll be able to handle them. You'll realize that you are bigger than they are.

Remember, conditions aren't always ideal in life. Stop fighting what is. Embrace your experience. This way you gather all your energies into your wholeness. Then what you thought was your enemy can become your ally, your friend.

Learning to accept and flow with what's happening leads you into one of the great secrets of healing and transformation: not to take your body—or yourself—so personally. True health is a balance of the impersonal with the personal, just as true happiness is a balance of outer, material security with inner, spiritual well-being.

Dispassionately observing the sensations and feelings in your body helps you develop the impersonal quality that is necessary if you want to feel your absolute best. The impersonal is the quality of detached global awareness in which there is space for tension to unwind and fresh, creative thinking to occur. The personal is the human element of feeling, love, affection. We need both the impersonal and the personal to be whole and happy. Find the balance.

Meditation—which, in essence, is just being very aware and present in the moment—develops the impersonal. It is the mental equivalent of sitting on the mountaintop, seeing clearly, viewing the big picture, getting perspective on life. Feeling your feelings, speaking the truth, and listening carefully to what others are saying to you develops the personal.

The impersonal is the background; the personal, the foreground. If you're too caught up in the foreground, the personal, you don't get the perspective you need to make the right decisions. You can't see the forest for the trees. Relationships become a source of emotional stress and conflict. When your body starts acting up, you panic.

On the other hand, if you're too identified with the background, the impersonal, you become too removed from life. You can no longer relate to people with the warmth and affection that are essential for healthy relationships. You become too detached from your body. When you withdraw your attention from your body, your life energy gets depleted and you start to have all kinds of health problems. No one is minding the store.

Cultivate impersonal awareness, embrace personal involvement. Find the balance between non-identification with your body and being *in* your body in a conscious, relaxed way.

## DRINK DEEPLY FROM YOUR OWN WELL

I'm not going to get into food and diet in this book, although obviously what you eat plays a major role in how clear and balanced you feel in terms of your own energy. You have to experiment with your food and take note of what it does for your energy level and how you feel after you eat.

The key to diet is to eat those foods which promote mental clarity, emotional harmony, and physical well-being (which includes maintaining your optimal weight), and to avoid those which make you feel tired, sluggish, and out-of-sorts. You can read books on food and nutrition, and experiment with any number of the suggested diets that are out there.

The best way to sort through the confusion around diets is to read your own internal book. Develop a relationship with your food. Notice how it makes you feel. Notice what it does to your energy. Food, ultimately, is just fuel, and you want to put the best possible (and best tasting!) fuel into your body—the high-octane stuff that allows your vehicle to perform at its absolute best for the longest time possible.

Food becomes such an issue for people because it serves all kinds of emotional needs, rather than just being fuel. Have you ever noticed that we live in a society where many of us have enough material security but are spiritually famished inside? Our souls are malnourished. We try to compensate for this emptiness by consuming endless quantities of food, stimulants, entertainment, goods, and so on. We've all done this at some point.

So why do we do it? Why do we keep looking for that "hit" of energy from outside when, deep down, we know it doesn't really fulfill us and never will? A certain amount of consumption, of seeking outside for our well-being, is clearly necessary. We all have a need for food, shelter, clothing, technology, and—most dear of all—friendship and love. But when we try and satisfy our inner spiritual hunger through outside sources, we just end up more hungry.

Eating disorders and habit problems—like the abuse of alcohol, drugs, or nicotine—are almost always a compensation, the result of a spiritual emptiness or longing. They are a sign that we are seriously out of balance. Address the imbalance, the spiritual longing, and the eating difficulty or negative habit will take care of itself. Notice that when you drink too much alcohol or eat the wrong kind of food at night, you usually feel lousy the next morning. Sometimes it can take a whole day before your energy gets clear and you start to feel reasonably human again.

It takes some people a few years—or a few decades!—of disturbing their energy in this way before they finally get the picture and start changing their drinking and eating habits. The key is to focus on your spiritual well-being. Having your energy feel good and clear over the long term will become more important than any short-term "high" or quick fix.

Beware of the consumer trap, of living with your attention fixed on the world outside you. It's difficult not to fall prey to this when you live in a consumer society like ours, with all its distractions and temptations.

In the consumer trap your mind becomes filled with thoughts, images, and pictures of the situations or circumstances—the "more"—that you hope or believe will bring you happiness. Your hopes and fantasies are fueled and fanned by the media, by advertising, and by continually watching and comparing yourself with other people.

Underneath this tide of hope and ambition, inevitably, is an undercurrent of doubt and fear—the fear that you won't be successful at what you do, the fear that you will never get what you want, the fear that if you do get it, the responsibility will be too much, or someone will come and take it away from you.

The danger of the consumer trap is that it causes you to become disconnected from what is authentic within you. It makes you forget how to relax and enjoy the fullness and flow of your own being. You start to lose the ability to delight in the simple realization that you are *enough* as you are, and that underneath all the mess and strife created by human beings there is extraordinary beauty and richness in life.

If you were to ask people how well they know themselves at a *being* level, many would probably just stare at you blankly or shake their heads in confusion. Their psychological and emotional identity, and thus their well-being, are pinned almost entirely to externals—to their circumstances, relationships, jobs, their place in society—and to the "story" they have created around all of this.

They are not at ease, they are not relaxed and at home in their own bodies. They don't know what it means to dive within and draw from the well of their own being for their happiness and security, which is what the experience of well-being really means. Indeed, whenever they stop long enough to notice what's inside their heart and soul, they usually encounter feelings of restlessness, emptiness, anxiety, and fear.

Their well-being has become almost wholly dependent on what is happening outwardly in their lives because of this lack of connection to their own inner wisdom and creative power. When there is money in the bank, when their job is secure, and when things are going well in their relationships, they are happy. If one of these conditions should go awry, however—if the money runs out, if the job is threatened, or if relationship problems erupt—then suffering and unhappiness ensue.

To avoid being in that shaky place where you are always at the mercy of circumstances, get acquainted with what's inside you. Love your body. Feel yourself *in* your body. Learn to drink deeply from the well of your own being. The guidance in this book will show you some very practical and effective ways of doing this, and of finding that inner state of balance and well-being that does not hinge solely upon externals.

## EASE AND BLISS

When you get really quiet and still, fully present in the moment, attuned to the subtlest movement of energy within and around you, the quickening life force causes a release of endorphins in your body. These are the hormones that dissolve pain and create pleasurable feelings, feelings of bliss, sometimes even ecstasy.

Bliss is what arises naturally when everything within you—body, mind, heart, soul—comes into perfect alignment or harmony. The energy of bliss is incredibly healing for the body. It softens, melts, and eventually eliminates all the physical blocks and imbalances that cause pain, stiffness, and inflammation. It brings a great sweetness to your life.

Tension and dis-ease are the result of a dominant sympathetic nervous system, the fight-or-flight response that is the chief trait of chronic anxiety. As you learn to let go and simply *relax,* the parasympathetic nervous system takes over and floods the body with warm, blissful feelings.

A good healer knows how to stimulate the flow of healing energy in the patient's body. As your consciousness evolves and expands, you learn to become your own healer. You learn how to move and flex your body to release tension and holding, and then how to get perfectly still, so that you can open up to the deeper flow of life energy, the bliss that is your true bodily nature.

As your wisdom ripens, you'll see that just as there is a wonderful upside to bliss, to the warm, melting sensations that you can create in your body, so there is also the danger of getting trapped by it. The bliss you get through moving your body, through making love, or through sitting in deep meditation and communing with the spiritual energy behind creation can become another addiction, just like any drug.

In time you'll find the balance. Bliss will be a place you visit periodically, whenever you need healing and renewal from within, whenever you need to drink from the well, the source of life, again. This may be once or several times a day, for a few minutes or for longer. Once you've made the connection, then it will be time to plunge back into everyday life and get on with the ever-important work of creating, relating, loving, and serving.

In any case, whenever you pause in your activities and consciously attune to the underlying rhythm and flow of the universe, bliss will be there. You'll feel it as the essence of your being, the very substance of who and what you are.

You'll notice that as you become more conscious and feel more at ease in your body, you'll bring through more life force. Your movements will be more graceful, and you'll radiate vitality. When you're not consciously connected to your body, you'll tend to move awkwardly, be clumsy, have accidents. If these things are happening to you, take heed. Be present. Be in your body.

You need some form of daily movement and stretching to help keep your body supple, to keep the energy moving through you. It doesn't take a lot, either. It's the quality of movement that counts, not the quantity.

There are many useful practices that foster conscious breathing, movement, and body-centering. They teach you how to move your own energy and stay grounded in your body.

Yoga, somatic (mind/body) exercises, dance, and martial arts are examples of such practices. Chiropractic, massage, body-work, and movement education are also good tools for helping you get more connected with your body. The more relaxed and present you are in your body, the less likely you are to be over-taken by fear, anger, depression, and other negative emotional states.

Remember, too, that it's not how your body looks that mat-ters. People get too hung up on images and appearances. Our society is filled with people who have shapely, buffed bodies, who wear the right clothes, live in the right houses, drive the right cars, have the right jobs, and yet are not happy. Their minds are filled with conflict and discontent, their hearts are empty, their souls are anguished, there's little or no love in their lives.

What really matters is how you feel in your body. By all means look your best (looking good is very much a part of the balance), but give even more attention to getting your internal energy flowing in a nourishing way. Start accepting the fact that there is really only one energy—the creative energy of life itself, the core vibration of the universe, the incredible and mysteri-ous power we call "spirit," "God," or "life force."

When you know how to relax and truly open up to it, you feel that vibration in your body as ease, bliss, well-being. You experience it in your mind as clarity, wisdom, meaning. You feel it in your heart as unity, love, joy.

Open up to who and what you truly are. Become a fine-tuned instrument for divine energy, for spiritual power. Let the energy of love shine through your eyes and through the pores of your skin. Then, no matter what others think of you, you'll feel good inside—and people will ultimately be attracted to that far more than they will to your outer appearances.

## HOW YOUR MIND AFFECTS YOUR BODY

There's an ancient Tibetan saying: "To see what you've done, look at your body. To see what you'll be, look at your actions."

Notice how when your body starts acting up, it drives you into your mind. For example, your stomach is upset, and it starts you thinking in negative ways. You begin to worry about having a serious illness, or you become obsessed with trying to eliminate or transcend the uncomfortable feelings.

Either way, you're thrown into mental conflict, and you become off-balance emotionally. You feel grumpy, out-of-sorts. Something is "eating" away at you. Not feeling good in your body is a major cause of mental and emotional suffering.

You can start to shift the energy by getting very present in your body and opening your heart to your discomfort. It's about having compassion for yourself. As you do this, and practice just observing the different sensations and feelings in your body, you become less caught up in them. When the judging mind stops interfering in your body's many processes, your body is free to find its own natural state of balance and harmony.

Illness, or malfunction, is fundamentally a disturbed energy pattern. You make the problem worse, however, when you start giving emotionally charged names to it. Even if you've been given a diagnosis of "cancer" or "arthritis," don't get too attached to the label. It only reinforces the belief that you are "sick."

Don't live in denial. Take whatever therapeutic measures may be necessary. But focus your attention on the deeper energy within you, your spirit. This is where you'll find the healing you seek. Learn to live in percepts, not concepts. Practice the art of pure perception, of being the consciousness, the space, in which objects appear, in which phenomena arise. This means simply being *aware* of what is instead of getting into your mind, with all its judgments and labels.

Very often, if you don't rush to name a disease—thereby giving it an "identity," a life of its own—the disturbed energy and sensations will sort themselves out and the feeling of well-being will return. The body, just like the universe itself, is a pulsating field of intelligence and creativity. Its own innate healing wisdom works marvelously well when you keep your ego—the interfering "I," with all its judgments and fears—out of the way.

Stay out of your mind, open your heart, listen to what your body is trying to tell you. Start noticing how conflicting thoughts and emotions manifest as stress and tension in the body, in both the organs and the muscles. Learning to relax inwardly helps you release this tension.

All your fears, defenses, and insecurities display themselves in unconscious patterns of tension and holding in your muscles and your posture. The more black-and-white you are in your thinking, the more rigid you'll be in your body. Your movements will be tense and stiff.

Issues around money and basic survival can manifest in problems in the low back, the power center in the body. Your support structure literally gives out. You're unable to move, to take any form of constructive action. In its extreme form, this inability to act is experienced as a kind of psychic paralysis. You feel powerless.

Sexual conflicts show up in a locked pelvis. The hips don't move freely or easily. Women with this problem often can't stand to be touched or even approached in that area. They become frigid, or unable to experience orgasm. Men who've relied so much on sexual fantasies that they're disconnected from their bodies become impotent, or else they suffer from premature ejaculation.

Relationship and emotional problems cause the belly to feel

all mushy, and then to tighten defensively. You find yourself saying, "My stomach hurts," or "My guts are in a knot."

Difficulties with self-acceptance, love, and living in the present manifest in the heart and mid-back. You feel a tightness in your chest, you have difficulty taking a deep breath, there's often a stabbing pain between your shoulder blades. A feeling of anxiety, even panic, can accompany these symptoms.

Blocked creativity and self-expression constrict the neck and throat. Chronic neck pain is often a sign that you are not being true to your self, that you are not honoring the call of your soul. Or you may find yourself coughing, choking up a lot. You're unable to articulate clearly. The truth you want to express won't come out. You may actually lose your voice.

Living too much in your head produces headaches, eye problems, dizziness, a "spaced-out" feeling. You feel scattered, ungrounded. You can't think straight much of the time. Underneath the obsessive need to get an intellectual grasp on life is a pervasive feeling of self-doubt.

If you have any of the physical symptoms just described, and they have failed to respond either to conventional or alternative treatment, it is time to explore the deeper issues that may be involved.

Face yourself honestly and ask yourself if you are experiencing emotional or personal issues related to the different areas of your body. Very often the sudden realization that you are really quite afraid of something, or that you have a lot of self-judgment, or that you are blocked creatively can itself open up a flood of new energy and, with it, the motivation to change.

If you need help in this process, consider working with a somatic therapist, someone who understands the relationship between energy, unresolved emotions, and the body. Better still, find one (they are out there) who has a transpersonal perspective and embodies, to some degree, the core insight. Such a practitioner will help you see where you're stuck in your own story, and they'll show you what is needed to get free of it.

It's important to gain insight into your emotional issues, and then learn to release the inner tension around them. Otherwise, what you hold on to will sooner or later have a negative impact on your well-being and make you feel very ungrounded.

## HEALING PAIN, ILLNESS, AND CONTRACTED STATES

You have probably observed that few things get your attention more than a sudden, unfamiliar ache, pain, or problem in your body. If you haven't yet developed a good relationship with your body, having something go wrong with it can be really scary.

When your back or some other part of your body starts acting up, instead of obsessively worrying about it—or, worse, cursing it—treat it like you would a friend or child who's hurting. Say to it things like, "Hey, what's the matter?" "How can I help?" "What do we need to do here?" Be kind, be supportive. If you must think something, think positive thoughts.

Listen carefully to the part of you that hurts, and it will speak to you through the voice of your intuition. Much of the time, unusual sensations or pain are transient, and will pass on their own. Your body was simply doing something to adjust itself internally as a way of relieving its own stress or tension.

If a problem persists, however, it may be a sign that you are out of balance in some way, and that you need to take corrective action. When an internal bodily stress or pain continues to gnaw at you, it's time to look at how you are living and if there's anything you need to change in your diet, exercise program, or the way you are relating to your work or to the people in your life. The great majority of health problems are stress-induced or stress-related.

Notice the feedback your body is giving you, make the connection between outer stress and physical and emotional tension, and then you'll have the information you need to make whatever internal adjustment or lifestyle changes might be appropriate.

There is another saying popular amongst alternative healers: if you can feel it, you can heal it. In other words, start really tuning in to the problem and you will get insight into it. But if you stay in denial around physical issues (or emotional ones, for that matter), if you refuse to face them, they persist—and often get worse.

Illness is a big stick. It can shock us into wakefulness. The trick is to learn to be really attentive at all times to what is going on in your body, and then you minimize the risk of getting "whacked" unexpectedly.

Of course, if ever your intuition is unclear when it comes to your health, seek out a wise and compassionate health practitioner. He or she will help you discover what's going on and what needs to be done about it.

Remember, too, that the body's energy, which includes sensations and feelings, is always in a state of movement. It is always seeking its own organic harmony. Stop labelling the sensations in your body "my bad back" or "my bum knee," and you give those contracted sensations called "pain" a chance to shift and change.

The most effective way to deal with pain or tension is to relax and breathe into it. Stay out of your head, out of judgments, labels, concepts, and simply breathe into the sensation. Open your heart to it.

Here is a powerful process for directing healing energy to those parts of your body that need it. I learned this from my friend John Allan, whose book, *The Healing Energy of Love,* deals a lot with the art of directing energy from a spiritual consciousness.

I use this technique whenever I experience persistent pain or illness of any kind. I am always amazed at how well it works. The more you practice the art of directing your awareness and intent in this way, the easier it is to do, and the more effective the results are. It is important, however, to let go of attachment to the results. Just focus on directing the energy in a very unconditional, loving way.

## TOOL #3
## DIRECTING HEALING ENERGY

Sit or lie down. Breathe consciously. Feel yourself slightly behind and above your head. Let your awareness expand, as you're now learning to do. Try and get a sense of your true nature, your real self, as being awareness, consciousness, expressing in this body/mind that is you. Your body may be ailing in some way, but who you really are—consciousness, or spirit, manifesting in this body/mind—is always perfect, whole, and healthy. Remember this.

Now bring your awareness into your heart. Breathe gently into your heart. Feel your heart soften, open, expand. Then visualize a current, a stream of warm, loving, healing energy moving from your heart out toward the injured or hurting part of your body. Breathe out as you do this. Literally "breathe" the flow of heart energy into the hurting area. Notice how, if you really relax into it, the heart energy softens and melts the hard, contracted places.

If you're working with an area of your body that burns or feels inflamed, visualize it being bathed with cool, soothing energy. You may also try this approach: focus your attention on an area of your body that feels light, open, expanded. With your eyes closed feel the energy there, then visualize it flowing toward—and gradually merging with—the painful area. Feel how the hurt area starts to soften and expand as it receives the new energy. Remember, the lighter, clearer energy always magnetizes and transforms the heavier, more dense energy.

Now come back to the sense of expansion, of expanded, or global, awareness. Let your breathing be soft, effortless. Let yourself be very still. With your heart still open, be thankful for the lessons to be learned from this bout of illness or pain you are experiencing. Remember, in every situation, even the most difficult one, there is a gift, a blessing. To discover it, to appreciate it and learn from it, is often the real beginning of healing.

---

Once you've learned how to direct energy for yourself, you can begin, if you wish, to do it for others who are sick or suffering in some way. Simply center and ground yourself, and then think of the person you want to direct energy to by holding the image of them in your mind. Then soften and open your heart, and direct a current or stream of energy from your heart to the person, visualizing it flowing toward them as you breathe out. You can also do this for pets or animals who are in trouble. Some people even do it for mechanical problems, like a car that won't start. Or for a business that needs more customers. Or for their empty bank account. It's amazing how energy works when you start opening to it!

The ability to move your own energy internally is also the secret of feeling young and vital, even as you age chronologically. You feel old when there's not much life energy moving through you. Your muscles and joints start to get stiff, your brain gets tired, your whole metabolism becomes fatigued. The key is to get the life energy—the endlessly creative and regenerative power of life itself—moving through you again. You do this through conscious breathing, movement, and a very heightened awareness of your body.

Take the needed time each day to contract, stretch, bend, move. Develop an exercise program that builds both strength *and* flexibility. Pause frequently to visualize the cells of your body expanding, opening up, allowing more energy through. The idea is to feel completely expanded and open inside, so that the incredible power of life itself can begin flowing through you, filling you with new energy, new vitality, new dynamism, new ideas, new possibilities.

Try it. You'll be amazed by what will happen!

## SERIOUS DISEASE

Sometimes an illness or disease can be so overwhelming or pervasive that its symptoms completely cloud your awareness and it is just impossible to open up to that feeling of clarity and expansion. If you are familiar with the pain of cancer, the constant wheezing or difficult breathing of a respiratory disease, or some other powerfully distracting or debilitating health problem, you will know what I mean.

If this is something you are dealing with, what can you do—especially when you consider that the medications you may be taking may actually dull your consciousness and make it even harder to be clear?

First, you have to address the problem therapeutically, whether it be through standard Western medical care, chiropractic, some form of alternative therapy (such as acupuncture, herbs, homeopathy, or Ayurvedic medicine), or a combination of several of these approaches. Do whatever you can to alleviate the worst of the symptoms.

Then it is really important to work with internal visualizations, such as the one I just shared with you, in order to practice moving your own energy from within. Remind yourself that all healing ultimately comes from inside you—that the power that made your body can heal your body.

And even if your body itself cannot be healed completely, your heart and soul can always be healed *totally,* because wholeness—peace, love, and inner joy—is your natural state. Even when you feel sick as a dog, you must keep remembering this. You must not let your faith in your true nature—the timeless wisdom and beauty inside you—ever wane. Hold to that, above all. Hold to the conviction that even though pain or some other form of distress may persist, you *will,* eventually, rediscover the inner serenity that is your true spiritual nature.

You may feel too much exhaustion and discomfort to actually meditate and clear your mind right away. Because of the mind/body connection, you may experience a tendency to slip all too easily into negative patterns of thinking. Trying to be philosophically detached from your illness just doesn't work. This is where it can get very difficult, but not impossible. Remember, many people have faced extreme physical discomfort but have been able to work through and transform their suffering with time, focus, and persistence.

Learning to live in awareness and acceptance of your body, mind, and senses creates more of a feeling of neutrality within you. It creates a sense of expansion, of new possibilities. Some of the charge is taken out of the physical problem. There is a diminishing of pain—even if just marginally—and a lessening of the worry, fear, and anger that may be associated with it.

With the dawning of even a little bit of clarity, you may find that you want to cut back on any medications that dull your awareness. You may find yourself more willing to put up with the pain, if it means that you can remain lucid and present, if it allows you to more easily tap into that larger spiritual reality beyond your limited physical circumstances.

It is a matter, as I have indicated, of beginning to trust and to accept that your real nature is bigger than your body, mind, and senses—and that even when your health may be utterly failing you, your inner spiritual core, that place within you of timeless awareness, peace, and love, remains untouched and inviolable.

Much of the rest of this book is devoted to giving you the information and inspiration that will allow you to draw closer to that trust and acceptance, until it becomes not just an idea but your actual and abiding reality. The wonder is that you can do this even though you may be dealing with a serious disease. In fact, for many people, it takes a major illness or some other crisis to launch them on the spiritual journey that is needed to bring their lives back into balance.

Many people in the New Age movement have been taught to believe that we create everything "negative" that happens to us, whether it is cancer, a car accident, or financial misfortune. I'd like to explore this line of thinking for a moment.

Such an attitude can, on the one hand, be very empowering. If you see yourself as the source of all you experience, and thus the ultimate cause of all your own problems, then you have it within you to find the solution. On the other hand, such a viewpoint can result in an enormous amount of guilt, accompanied by feelings of victimhood and hopelessness. And it doesn't begin to explain why some unfortunate babies are born with terrible diseases or infirmities.

My own intuitive understanding around this issue is that we certainly create many of our own problems—perhaps as much as seventy to eighty percent—because of mental and emotional stress and "human error" such as poor choices, ignorance, and negligence in matters of health.

But a good twenty to thirty percent is due to causes over which we may have little or no control. These include heredity and other genetic factors (in the case of disease, the body has its own conditioning, its own inherited karma to work out); physical trauma and injury; toxins, pollutants, and carcinogens in our water, food, and environment; and maybe even some plain bad luck once in a while.

What you, as a conscious human being, do have control over is your *response* to the disease. Your initial reaction may be one of upset, and even a feeling of being victimized. But, as you remember to breathe, and come back to the clarity and power of the present moment, you can begin to see your situation in a different light.

Treat your illness, your suffering, as an opportunity for spiritual transformation, and I guarantee that you will learn and grow from it. You may even discover that within the seeds of this unfortunate, even wretched, event, lies an unexpected blessing, an opportunity to deepen your faith in, and contact with, your spiritual core.

But if you persist in seeing the disease as an unwanted curse, and yourself as a victim, you will just perpetuate your suffering, and you will get even further disconnected from the beauty and wisdom of your heart and soul.

### FINE-TUNING THE INSTRUMENT

It becomes clear how chronic physical knots and emotional blocks prevent the energy, the life force, from flowing easily through your cells. Like water that just collects, your energy stagnates. Over time you experience this stagnation of energy as fatigue, weariness, a lack of creativity. It's one of the main causes of feeling old before your time.

Remember to keep the life energy moving through you. This is the way to always feel young, even as you age chronologically. Let yourself become free in body and mind. Don't cling to anything. Through learning to sense and feel the unconscious patterns behind the stress in your body, you start to release them.

At the beginning of this chapter I talked about the body as a vehicle for your spirit, the being you really are. Another good metaphor is to think of your body as an instrument. If you are a musician and you want to perform at your best, you must play with a fine-tuned instrument.

Consider a guitar, for instance. If the strings are too loose, you can't get a decent sound out of them. If they are too tight, you risk having a string break. There is a midpoint, the balance point, where the tension is just right. Not too little, not too much. Then you can play the most exquisite music.

When you fine-tune your physical instrument through exercise, conscious eating, relaxation, and the practice of being very present in the moment, then you can get the most energy and pleasure out of it. You ensure the highest degree of health. You sleep much better. Indeed, the more awake you are during the day, the better you sleep at night. The more "asleep" you are during the day—the more caught up in your mind, in your story—the more you lie awake at night, tossing, turning, fretting.

Karlfried Graf Durckheim, a German psychotherapist and spiritual master, once said that a neurotic is a person who can't find himself in his body. Neurotics are so "personally" identified with, or attached to, everything that happens to them that it drives them crazy. They are unable to effectively tune their own instruments because they are so disconnected from them. Consequently, such people frequently suffer a host of physical problems, energy disturbances, and illnesses.

To some degree, we all have tendencies toward imbalance or neurosis. It comes with the territory of being human. We all walk, at times, a fine line between sanity and madness, never quite knowing when something might happen to push us over the edge. This is why we have to be so aware, so highly attuned to our bodies, to the unfolding energy of the moment. Then we can make the necessary adjustments to keep ourselves centered and grounded.

Developing a more impersonal awareness of the ever-changing phenomena in your mind and body helps you get more perspective on what is going on inside you. It gets you out of the loop, so to speak. You're no longer so caught up in transient events and effects. This naturally leads to an increased feeling of ease and well-being.

It's overidentification with the body that breeds so much fear. When you don't know yourself at a spiritual level, you'll inevitably feel afraid when your body starts acting up. Your very sense of "self" will feel threatened.

Your body, mind, and senses naturally come into harmony and balance when "you"—the controlling "I," or ego—get out of your own way, and are simply present as unconditional awareness. Then, when the body goes through its ups and downs, as it will from time to time, you won't take it so personally. You focus instead on creating expansion, space inside your own consciousness, and then your body has room in which to balance and heal itself. Consciousness itself, you begin to realize, is the healing and transformative agent. The more conscious you are, the more whole you feel.

Freedom from the ego's grip is the real key to happiness and well-being. This is the core insight, the one essential truth that all awakened people understand. Stop taking yourself to be "somebody," learn to look at life without the "me" in the way, and you'll come to the same understanding. You'll see and experience reality as it is. You'll tap into the fundamental unity, beauty, and sacredness of life.

In the end, your body is going to die. Like a suit of old

clothes, it's going to drop away. This thought is less scary as you get more in touch with your true spiritual nature—which is timeless, beyond birth and death. How to do that is what the spiritual quest, the journey of self-knowing, is all about. As you go deeper on your journey, you'll get freer of fear and limitation.

Love your body, but don't be too attached to it. Honor it, but don't make an idol of it. Take good care of it, and it will take good care of you. Happy are those who have their feet planted firmly on the ground and are fully and strongly present in their bodies!

Remember: relax, stay loose, *breathe.* Develop a conscious and dynamic relationship with your body, and it will be much easier to master everything else you need to learn to walk the inner path and bring your life into balance.

CHAPTER TWO

# Clearing Your Mind

### THE KEY TO CLARITY

*I*t can't be said enough: the body and mind are not separate. What happens to your body affects how you think, and vice versa. If you eat too much, you feel uncomfortable, and it clouds your ability to think clearly. If you start having fearful thoughts, you feel a contracting of the energy in your body.

Prolonged worry stresses the body and can cause a host of problems. However, if you understand the mind/body relationship, you have the key to eliminating psychosomatic disease. Understanding itself brings clarity to the mind. Without clarity, thinking gets confused and causes emotional upset.

Don't, however, confuse clear thinking with analysis. People who are too analytical get stuck in their heads. They are usually very tight in their bodies, stiff in their movements, controlled in their behavior and actions. Such people are often referred to as being "anal." You might even say, anal-ytical! They can get so bound up in words and concepts that they become mentally constipated. Don't let that happen to you!

The trick is to not waste energy in unnecessary thinking. Be aware, be open, be present. Learn to use thought when needed.

It is a marvelous creative tool. But don't miss life, the fullness of the moment, by always being in your head.

Clear seeing is not the same as positive thinking, either. Positive thinking is a decision to see things in a particular way, regardless of how they actually may be. This can be useful up to a point. It's certainly more constructive to think positively than negatively. If you are facing a challenging situation, it will serve you better to look for the gift, the lesson, the blessing in it, rather than getting caught up in thoughts of hopelessness and despair.

Positive thinking only becomes a limitation when it is used to cover up or overcome your ego's insecurities, when it reinforces the notion of a "self" who needs to view life in a particular way in order to be happy. Then it can keep you stuck in the belief that you're not enough as you are. You have to continually generate positive thoughts to feel okay.

Too much thinking of any kind makes you overly mental. It keeps you in your head and prevents you from opening fully to the wisdom in your heart, to the deeper energy of the moment. Scratch the surface of a person who's made a religion out of positive thinking, and you'll often find someone in a lot of inner turmoil. There's often a lack of authenticity, of spontaneity in such people.

There's another problem that comes from being too mental. I once heard a speaker refer to it as the most common mental disease in our culture: psychosclerosis, or hardening of the mind. Hardening of the mind leads to being overly serious. The antidote, clearly, is to lighten up!

It's important to differentiate, however, between serious-earnest and serious-grim. The former is necessary for success in life. A certain earnestness, an intensity of desire and focus, is essential if you are to attain anything worthwhile. But serious-grim just gives you hemorrhoids and takes all the joy out of living.

A good way to know if you are too caught in your head (other than friends telling you) is to notice if you have any facial tension. If your cheeks or eyes feel tense, if you're experiencing any kind of a facial twitch or tic, it may mean you're thinking too much. Be thankful for such internal feedback. Pay attention to it. Shift the energy by breathing deeply, feeling your feet on the ground, and centering yourself. Visualize yourself sending your energy down from your head, into your belly, your legs, the earth.

To see clearly is to see things as they are, without the interference of your mind. It's to see without all the filters of thought, belief, emotional programming. An image that can help you come to greater clarity is that of the movie projector. If you imagine the circumstances of your life as a movie played out on the screen, then think of your mind as the film and your awareness as the light in the projector.

Whatever is in your mind gets projected out onto the screen that is life. If you have fearful, anxious thoughts, you tend to create circumstances that give you cause for worry and fear. If you are a woman who has had bad experiences with men, then every time you meet a man, the negative memories in your mind will tend to be projected out onto the new man. If you are a man who has a lot of unresolved internal conflict with his mother, then every time you meet a woman and sense any emotional connection, you'll tend to project your mother's face onto this new woman.

All this is done subconsciously, of course. The way to begin to transform the circumstances of your life is to start clearing the film. You do this by becoming more *aware* of the thoughts in your mind. You amplify the light, so to speak.

This is how meditation serves you. As your awareness shines more clearly and brightly, it dissolves, burns out, the old images on the film—all the negative, limiting "stuff" from your past. There is more room in your mind for fresh, creative, focused thinking. Your mind naturally thinks positively when it's operating from a clear, ego-free place. Then you can begin to create a new movie, one that reflects who you really are, and that expresses what you truly want to do with your life.

Use thought, but don't be run by it. You have a mind, but you are not your mind. You are the awareness in which your mind appears. Remembering this is the key to clarity.

## STATES OF MIND

If you really start to pay attention, you'll notice that most of the thoughts passing through your mind are the same thoughts that passed through it yesterday—and the day before. Just to be aware of this fact can be liberating. The realization that you are wasting energy in unnecessary thinking can itself bring the mind to silence.

As you train your awareness in this way, which is what meditation is all about, your mind has less and less power over you. You start to be in charge of it, instead of it controlling you.

Boredom, guilt, worry, confusion, depression, and fear are all states of mind. When you live in your mind, in endless thinking about yourself and your problems, these states are inevitable. Let's take a closer look at them, at how they arise, how they persist, and how you can begin to free yourself from them.

**Boredom** sets in when your mind runs out of stimulating ideas, fantasies, things to think about, to do, to look forward to. If you live in your mind, the risk of boredom will always loom large in your awareness. This is why children—and teenagers, especially—get bored so easily in our culture. They have been accustomed to such a constant bombardment of stimulation that, when it lets up, they don't know what to do with themselves.

The cure for boredom is not to scout around for yet something else that is new and stimulating, for that just perpetuates the problem. Rather, it is to come back to the present, to your breath, to sensation to feeling. When you live in your body and open your heart and mind to the fullness of the moment, boredom is never a problem. Life, creation, is endlessly new and interesting.

**Guilt** is the result of judging yourself harshly for past errors and mistakes, and then holding on to an image of yourself as being "bad" or "unworthy." To get free of guilt, you have to eliminate moral considerations and look from a purely practical, functional perspective at the situation that is triggering the guilt.

For example, let's say you told a lie to someone, and now you feel bad about it. You feel guilty. First, see that feeling guilty is essentially a way of beating yourself up mentally and emotionally. It's just another story to tell yourself—"I guess I'm a bad person"—that keeps you from being the wise, loving, and beautiful person you really are.

In terms of the lie, if it's relatively unimportant and there isn't likely to be any fallout, you simply resolve not to do it again, knowing that lying doesn't work. It creates too much of a burden that you then have to carry around, as you try and remember to keep your "story" straight every time you speak to this person.

The best course, however—especially if this person really is your friend—is to come clean and confess. Apologize. Tell the person you don't know what got into you. (Usually it's because you didn't want to hurt his or her feelings, or have him or her think badly of you.)

The critical step in freeing yourself from guilt is to stop being so personally attached to everything you've done, or that's happened to you. See that guilt itself is an unnecessary encumbrance, one that only leads to uncomfortable feelings of embarrassment and shame, and thus is a detriment to your spiritual well-being. Learn from your mistakes, make whatever amends need to be made, then let the past go.

**Worry, confusion,** and **fear** arise in a mind restlessly looking for a foothold, some kind of certainty to which it can cling—and despairing because it can find none. Again, if you live in your mind, there will always be plenty to worry about. There will be no end to all the potentially horrible scenarios and outcomes you can imagine. Sometimes, there is just so much conceptual data coming in from so many directions that you don't know which to accept, and which to reject.

The most effective way to transform the energy of worry, confusion, and fear is to come down out of your head, breathe, and center yourself in your body, in the present moment. Let go of your agendas, the attachment to your story. Just be present. Wait, and trust. The information or understanding you need will come to you. You'll know what, if anything, you need to do.

**Depression** sets in when your mind is so closed-off to life and its infinite possibilities that your feelings shut down. You become numb, listless. There's a strong sense of futility, despair, hopelessness. At its most pervasive, depression is the soul crying out for God, the divine. An inflated sense of self, of ego, can also lead to depression—to a deflation of "self." From this perspective, depression is collapsed pride.

In chapter 7, I relate the story of how I faced my own feelings of depression and, as a result, broke through to a whole new level of freedom. People who have been diagnosed as being clinically depressed may well need medication to help them through the worst of it. But for the rest of us, those dealing with the more common "existential depression," there is a very viable solution.

The immediate answer is to get moving, to exercise the body, to engage in creative activity to raise your level of energy from its depressed—or "pressed down"—state. But the long-term cure for depression, as well as boredom, guilt, worry, fear, and other negative states, is self-knowledge.

Find out who you are beyond your mind, beyond all your ideas and images about who you are, and freedom will become very real and alive for you.

## YOU ARE NOT YOUR THOUGHTS

When you're ready, start probing beneath the surface. Look for the source of thought itself. Where does it come from? How does it arise? What triggers it? Don't make this an intellectual exercise—another mind game—but actually *do* it. This is real meditation.

Try and pinpoint the home of your mind, and you won't be able to find it. That's because the mind is nonlocal in nature. It's everywhere. It reaches into every part of your body, and beyond.

You can prove this for yourself. You can move your awareness down into the big toe of your right foot. Notice the quality of sensation and feeling there, and then begin to visualize heat. Actually feel your big toe warming up as you concentrate an intensity of warmth there. Even go so far as to see it being on fire, getting really hot. Do this for a minute or two, then reach down with your fingers and feel the actual difference in temperature between the left big toe and the right.

Or you can take an object like a flower, and meditate on it with your eyes open. Project your awareness into the flower. See the petals opening, peeling back, inviting you in as they would a bee coming to pollinate. If you really let your awareness be absorbed by the flower, you may find that "you" actually disappear into it. You become one with it, until there is just the flower, its petals opening and dancing in your awareness, its colors dazzling you, its fragrance subtly overwhelming you.

The mind, you begin to realize, is not just thought. It's much more than that. It's the faculty of perception as well—watching, sensing, feeling, listening, touching, tasting. Perception has no limits; you cannot localize the mind, but you *can* localize thought. If you pay attention, you'll notice that the center of most of your thinking is in the frontal lobe of your brain, slightly above and behind your eyes. Thought arises from behind that place known as the "third eye."

Begin to notice the fact that thoughts are *objects,* just like birds, trees, or automobiles. Regular sitting meditation (see the next tool) will help reinforce this awareness, but for now, just play with the notion that even though thoughts are ephemeral, insubstantial mind "flashes," they are still objects.

Why? Because you can *observe* them, just as you can observe a bird or a tree. You can watch a thought arise out of nowhere—for example, "I must call my mother," or "What am I going to do next weekend?"—and you can watch it recede into the emptiness from whence it came.

If you can observe, or watch, a thought come into existence and then disappear again in this way, even such a personal thought as "I," it demonstrates a very fundamental truth: you cannot *be* the thought. Rather, you are that which is doing the observing. Now, sit with *that* realization for a minute or two!

The discovery that you are not your thoughts but rather are the awareness behind them is, quite literally—no pun intended—a mind-blowing insight. It brings you to a deep inner silence, which allows you to look at the world, at your whole material situation, with new eyes. You see how so much of what you take to be "reality" has been created out of the thoughts you think, and how much power this understanding gives you to create a new reality.

For many people, chaos seems to be a necessary prelude to creativity. It seems to be the only way they can come up with new ideas—by going through a whole lot of confusion and struggle first. But there is a much more efficient and harmonious way to access creative thinking, and that is through a quiet, clear mind. When the mind is relatively empty of thought, not only do you see reality as it is—without the filters and biases—but also new energy is unleashed, generating a wave of fresh, innovative, and focused thinking.

And the way to access this state is to remember who you are, to remember that awareness *always* precedes thinking. So, why not live from the source? Why not live from awareness itself? This is what the core insight is really about.

As you open up to the awareness that is your true nature, don't worry about trying to still your mind totally. Given that the mind's nature is movement—it's a thought-producing instrument, a biocomputer—to try to have no thoughts at all is to miss the point. Just learn how to slow them down through continually coming back to the awareness *behind* thought.

As you learn to let your mind slow down even further—through just watching it, through not getting caught up in thinking and thus giving thought undue power—a day will come when you'll pop free altogether. You'll actually experience thought releasing its grip on you.

It's quite an amazing thing when this happens. You're obsessing about something and then you realize what you are doing. You stop, breathe, feel your connection to the earth. You start listening to the sounds around you, you notice the clouds above. A bird alights nearby and starts chirping. Then, bingo! Suddenly, you're in present time. You're not caught up in your mind any longer. Then you can think about anything, and thoughts are no longer a problem.

This is when you feel the connection to an energy much bigger than you. A universal energy. And you realize you *are* this energy. You are a unique, individualized expression of it.

You may only be in this awareness for a few minutes, but once you've had a taste of it, it is easier to find your way back. Inside yourself you have an organic memory of wholeness, of freedom, and it is this memory that calls you home, that brings you back to who you really are.

From this place of global, or expanded, awareness you can *use* thought, but you won't be used by it. You'll be in charge of your mind, not controlled by it. Then you can really begin to tap its creative powers.

With the slowing down of your mind, paradox will cease to be a problem for you, as will contradiction. When people live from their minds, they demand certainty. Things have to be either black or white. Shades of gray are threatening, and mystery is downright unsettling. But when you're no longer at the mercy of your mind, then there's room enough for everything. While you appreciate intellectual clarity, you don't need intellectual certainty, simply because you don't live from your intellect. You use it as a tool, but you don't cling to intellectual, analytical thinking as a way of life.

It's a great freedom to be able to sit, to breathe, to be. To be so open, empty, that the whole movement of life—all its drama, its ordinariness, its pain, its joy—can wash right through you, and not carry you away.

From this space you notice ever more clearly how your body, senses, and thoughts appear *within* the field of your awareness. You don't so much live in your body, as your body lives in you. Your real nature, you intuit, is this nonlocal awareness expressing itself in this unique body/mind complex that is "you."

The more attuned you are to your real nature, the more you see everything with a balanced perspective. Balanced seeing, in turn, leads to right action—and right action results in harmonious living.

## THE POWER OF MEDITATION

If the core insight is seeing that you are not your "story," but the awareness behind it, then meditation is the core *practice*. It is meditation that clears the clutter and debris from your mind and paves the way for the core insight. It brings you to the place where you can see yourself and your life with total clarity.

To meditate is to sit and be present with whatever is happening. When you first learn to sit and formally meditate, it can be difficult because all your "stuff" tends to come up. You may experience physical tension and pain, boredom, restlessness, anxiety, confusion, fear, loneliness.

Facing all this in yourself is part of what meditation is about. You learn to breathe through these difficult states, and eventually they pass and cease being a problem. You find yourself arriving at deeper levels of clarity, stillness, and peace. You come to your own realization of the truth contained in the following *haiku,* which I penned while meditating on my deck one morning at sunrise:

> *Supremely present, mind still*
> *I breathe in*
> *The beauty of this moment*

Many people struggle with meditating and attaining a quiet mind, yet it can happen with surprising ease and spontaneity.

Another story about my son, Adam, will illustrate what I mean.

He was about eleven years old at the time. Although he often saw me meditate in the morning if he got up early enough, he rarely, if ever, "sat" formally himself. We occasionally talked about spirituality and enlightenment, but mostly I just let him enjoy being a kid. His basic nature was (and is) kind, loving, and generous. He was a happy child who was in touch with the "energy" behind creation. How much more spiritual could you get? The last thing I needed or wanted to do was lay any spiritual "trip" on him.

On this particular occasion we were on a hike in the hills near where we live. It was a beautiful summer's day, and it was hot. We were walking along a wide dirt trail that wound its way through some woods and out into an open meadow, when we decided to stop for a break. I was about twenty yards ahead of him. He plopped himself down right in the middle of the trail, under the trees. I had just come out into the open and had found a comfortable rock to sit on. I had pulled out my water bottle and was taking a drink, watching a turkey vulture wheeling overhead, when he called out.

"Dad!" he said, excitedly.

"What?" I turned to face him.

"I just meditated!"

"What happened?" *Now,* this *is going to be interesting,* I thought.

He proceeded to tell me. "Well, I sat down and my mind was jumping with all kinds of thoughts, and I just started to really notice these trees, and how the wind was blowing the leaves around. Then I could hear the wind. Then I heard some kind of a bird singing. . . . And then guess what happened?"

"What?"

"My mind just stopped!"

"And . . . ?"

"Well, everything just stopped. Like, I just got completely quiet inside."

"How did that feel?"

"It felt *great!*" He jumped up and came over to me, thrilled at this new discovery. "Man, now I can meditate!"

"You sure can," I said, putting my arm around his shoulder and giving him a hug.

As we continued our walk along the trail, I said to him, "So now you know what to do. You've learned the secret of meditation. Whenever you feel scattered or need to recharge yourself, you just sit down and get really still. Then you simply pay attention to what you see in your immediate environment, and you listen carefully to the sounds you hear, and suddenly you find yourself out of your head, and you're right here in the moment."

"It feels great to be in the moment, Dad."

"You're still a kid, Adam," I replied, "so you're there pretty naturally. Just remember what happened today, and you'll always know how to get back to the now moment if ever you get lost in your mind again."

Let me share with you now the specific meditation practice that has worked so well for me for more than twenty years. It is a practice that quickly releases any fuzziness or static in my mind, as well as fatigue or stress in my body. Within a few minutes it usually brings a wonderful feeling of alignment in body, mind, and spirit.

I sit every morning, for ten or fifteen minutes if I have a lot of writing or other work to get to, for thirty or forty minutes when I have more leisure time. Sometimes, I'll also sit for a little while in the evening, although I usually do my half-hour yoga practice in the evening. That is more of a moving meditation—a balancing of dynamic poses, with periods of total stillness in between.

The movement of the yoga releases the accumulation of the day's stress; the stillness in between the poses allows me to feel the exquisite energy that bubbles up in every cell, the delightful current of bliss that is the by-product of deep and profound relaxation.

## TOOL #4
## MEDITATION

Choose a meditation environment where you feel a sense of peace, quiet, and beauty. Sit comfortably, either in a chair or on a cushion, with your back straight. Close your eyes, breathe down into your belly. Feel yourself in your body. Feel yourself centered, grounded, solid. Be supremely present.

Using the Expanding Awareness technique you learned in chapter 1, visualize yourself as being the awareness, the space, in which your body appears, in which your breath rises and falls, in which sensations come and go. As you let your awareness expand even further, listen to the sounds around you—whether of an electrical appliance, a car going by, the wind sighing, or a bird calling. Then tune in to the silence behind the sounds. The deep silence out of which all sounds arise, and back into which they disappear. Notice how the silence, the stillness, is always here—and that it is both empty and incredibly full, rich in creative potential. When you are totally present like this, you discover that there is always something new being born out of silence.

As you observe, or witness, the continual flow of sensations and feelings in your body, start paying attention to the thoughts and images in your mind. Watch them as you would birds flying across the sky in front of you. Just watch them and let them fly by, whether they are thoughts of past events, of people in your life, or of what might happen in the future. Don't go chasing after them. Don't indulge yourself in "thinking" about them. This meditation time is your opportunity to experience what it is like to be free of thoughts of the past and future, and simply be here in the present.

So, as you sit, just focus on the sense of your true nature as being awareness, the vast, clear blue sky, and your thoughts are but birds winging their way overhead. Experience the marvelous freedom of not holding on to *anything* but instead, just being fully present with your awareness.

Periodically, open your eyes so as to reconnect with your immediate surroundings. It will help you stay present. Coming back to the awareness of your breath, to slow, conscious breathing, will also help. Remember, the primary goal of meditation is to simply be very still, very present, very alert and attuned to whatever is unfolding in this moment now.

(When you start to experience more peace and serenity in your meditation, you can begin to use your new clarity to explore issues and problems you may be dealing with. I'll talk more about how to do that later in this chapter, under the section titled Negative Energy.)

---

As your sitting meditation practice deepens and you become more comfortable with it, states of tension, restlessness, and boredom will be less and less of a problem. You'll breathe into them, and they will pass. A marked sense of ease, clarity, and well-being will more and more be your steady experience.

There is an extremely critical point to be aware of here, too. The failure to understand it is, in my experience, one of the main reasons why true freedom continues to elude so many people. It is this: as you learn to release attachment to thoughts by simply witnessing them, you must apply this process to every thought that arises, whether it's a pleasurable thought, an uncomfortable thought, or a neutral thought.

The mistake many people make is that they try and let go of the so-called negative thoughts while continuing to indulge the pleasant ones. This is understandable enough at a certain level. If thinking particular thoughts makes you feel good, why give them up? But there is a pitfall here. Because of the mind's dual nature—the way it thinks in opposites—you can't entertain a positive thought without there being a negative, contradictory one lurking somewhere in the background.

Whether you're clinging to something from the past that feels good, or a thought that makes you look forward to some imagined future, you can be sure there are equally potent negative thoughts (having to do with pain, or the fear of loss or failure) not far away. But as you get free of *all* psychological and emotional thinking through meditation, space opens up in your mind, and thought can be used for the powerful tool it is—in a fresh, creative, and inspiring way.

Meditating with closed eyes helps shut out external stimuli. You're less distracted. It's easier to get quiet and still within, to observe your body, senses, and mind. Meditation is not meant to be an escape, however, or a tranquilizer.

Some people like to go off on an internal "trip" when they meditate—a fantasy, a mental vacation. There's nothing wrong with this, but it won't lead you to true freedom. If you want to be free so that you can live in the world with real inner balance, you have to learn to be totally present, with all your attention. Using the meditation tips I am sharing with you here will help you do that. It will help you get freer of your psychological and emotional baggage, so that you can be more present, more aware, more mindful.

Opening your eyes periodically during meditation reminds you to be here now. It gives you the experience of being totally connected with your environment, with the reality of the present. Driving, for instance, is a great meditation—and you need your eyes open for that! You need to be fully present when you drive. You cannot afford to internally "trip" or space out.

Eventually, as inner stillness becomes easier and more natural for you (and this inner clarity and ease is your natural state), you'll bring that meditative awareness into everything you do, even when you're negotiating or trading in the hurly-burly of the marketplace.

Once sitting meditation starts to become easier and more natural for you, it will then be necessary (if you want to be *really* free) to begin to inquire, "So, who meditates?" It's about looking deeply within to find out who this "I" is, just who you take yourself to be. This is where you start to face the core insight, where you start to really peel away the layers of the onion that has been the "story" of your life.

You can begin the process of self-inquiry by practicing the art of looking, listening, and feeling without naming or labelling whatever you are experiencing. Be open to whatever is passing through your awareness without getting caught up in words and concepts. It's the quickest way to see through your own ego and its attachments, and come to peace and harmony.

Then go even further. Try listening without being "somebody" who listens. In other words, let yourself be totally absorbed by what you hear, so that you're not even thinking, "I'm hearing this." Just be in total openness.

In the same way, practice feeling the sensations in your body without being conscious of "yourself" as someone who is feeling. Then try looking at objects without thinking of yourself as the "looker." Doing all this will help you release the attachment to "I," "me," and "mine," and will bring you closer to true freedom.

As you grow quieter and your mind clears through meditation, your awareness will become global, multidimensional. You will feel extremely alert, present, aware of everything that is happening around you—to the front, to the sides, above, below.

This is what the term "global" means. Your awareness literally extends in every direction, horizontally, vertically, and reaches out—it seems—to infinity. And it is all happening right here, right now. All your senses are alive, and the moment itself becomes incredibly rich and full. This is where meditation leads you.

## DEALING WITH INTENSE FEELINGS AND EMOTIONS

When you're in the grip of intense feelings or emotions, there's nothing to do but feel them. You certainly can't "think" your way out of them—or if you do, it usually just results in repression or denial, and then you face the risk of illness and other somatic symptoms.

Bob Hoffmann, in his book, *No One Is to Blame,* summed it up neatly when he said, "Reason is a tiny ship on the ocean of emotion." Feeling and emotions come in waves, sometimes gentle, sometimes intense. The best way to deal with them is to just breathe into them, ride them, don't fight them. The ocean that is emotion will soon calm down, and peace will prevail. Eventually, clarity and understanding will come.

Emotions are strong feelings. Authentic emotion is spontaneous in the way it arises and passes. You see this with young children. Young children don't yet have a strongly developed personal sense of self, or ego, to cling to hurt feelings. They intensely feel and express their pain or upset, and then they are done with it. They are happy again.

The less "I," or ego, there is, the more quickly strong emotions such as grief and anger pass. A Zen master—or any adult who has awakened to the core insight—experiences emotion in the same spontaneous, authentic way that a child does. You feel it, express it, and then it is over.

Anger is toxic when it comes from the ego. The ego's anger is *self*-righteous, as in "How dare you do this to *me!*" Healthy anger is free of the "me." It arises as an immediate response to injustice, to behavior that threatens human life and well-being. This is righteous anger, the anger of God, of truth, of the divine within you. It takes whatever action is needed to correct the injustice, and then it dissolves again.

Anger and power are connected. If you can't express your anger, you won't be able to connect with your power. If you're struggling with feelings of powerlessness, start owning your anger. You'll feel less like a victim. You'll start to feel genuinely empowered.

In general, feelings are just feelings, flowing sensations in the body that, if associated with an image or memory of some kind, become emotions. You can experience feelings of lightness, ease, expansion, contraction, or heaviness that don't have any particular association. They just are what they are.

But when an association is triggered in your consciousness, feeling becomes emotion. For example, the loss of someone you love brings up the emotion of grief. A deliberate or malicious betrayal triggers the emotion of anger. Holding on to feelings of guilt results in shame. On the positive side, an act of spontaneous generosity provokes the emotion of joy.

Emotions, then, are thought-based. Upsetting thoughts breed upsetting emotions. Learn to stay out of your mind— think only when you need to think!—and you'll experience a more consistent emotional harmony and stability.

It's not thoughts themselves that create conflict. It's the emotional attachment to them. It's constantly thinking about the past that keeps the painful aspects of it alive. The practice of meditation as I've outlined it in this chapter—with the emphasis on being fully alert in the present—will free you from the past. As you learn to observe, or witness, images and pictures arising from your past, they will tend to just drop away, and the emotional charge around them will dissolve.

Feelings are just feelings, but emotions tend to be more personal. The more *self*-centered you are, the more emotional conflict you'll experience. For proof of this, just think of someone you know who seems to be in emotional upset a lot. Invariably, you will find that most of their conversation revolves around themselves, their problems, and how mean or selfish other people are, and how difficult and unfair life is.

It is a classic victim's stance, and behind it there is usually some core sense of being "wronged" by someone or something in the past. The past wound or hurt festers in the person's psyche and blurs his or her judgment in so many matters. Put all your emotional eggs in one basket, and you're liable to end up a basket case!

There's no moral judgment here (we've all felt victimized at times), but thinking of yourself as a victim is disempowering. It won't produce the results you want. The feeling of being a victim is one of the main mind-sets that stops people from accessing and realizing their inner potential for happiness and success.

There is a clear prescription for finding emotional balance and harmony: start letting go of attachment to images and ideas of "self," to the concepts "I," "me," and "mine." It really is that simple! (It is not easy, I admit, which is why we need to read books like this, and practice meditation, and the art of self-inquiry, in order to come to true inner freedom.)

All emotion gets expressed in the body. Withheld emotions manifest as stress and tension in the neuromuscular system. It's important not to suppress feelings and emotions—and not to dump them on others, either.

Emotional moods, whether it's lingering sadness, depression, or resentment, are like a train. They come seemingly out of nowhere. They pull in at the station that is your mind, pluck you right off the platform of your awareness, and, before you know it, you're off for a rocky or distressing ride.

The more centered you are, the more clearly you see the "mood" train approaching. You're able to step back and hold your ground, and breathe into the thought, feeling, or sensation so that you don't get taken along with it.

I remember a session in therapy many years ago when I was feeling a lot of pain around the breakup of my marriage. I was crying pretty intensely, and then, suddenly, I became *aware* of myself crying. It was an unusual experience, and marked an important signpost on the road to freedom for me. I was able to witness, observe—from a clear, unconditional space—my personal "self" going through its deep suffering.

Previously, whenever I felt emotional pain, I was always totally identified with it. I *was* the sadness, the fear, the confusion. But this time, I fully experienced my anguish and, simultaneously, watched myself experiencing it.

When I left the session that day, I felt marvelously cleansed on a personal level because I had allowed the feelings to be fully expressed, and yet I had not taken them personally, as I usually did. Thereafter, whenever emotion came up for me for any reason, I could feel it *and* be fully aware of it at the same time.

Enlightened therapists bring this transpersonal perspective to their work. They want you to know and experience yourself at a personal level, but they will also constantly remind you of who you really are, and guide you away from getting stuck in the personal.

The key is to feel the feelings but not get into your head about them. Don't analyze them. Just be aware. Be aware that your true nature *is* awareness, the timeless and impersonal presence behind the story, behind all the mental and emotional drama that is part of the human scene. Then, no matter how intense the feelings are, they won't sweep you away. You'll experience the energy and the passion of them, but they won't diminish or distract you from your inner clarity.

In the end, there's nothing to do with intense feelings and emotions but to breathe into them, and to feel them. Then the energy behind them can shift, move, evolve into something new.

An encounter I had with Adam illustrates this. He was upset to the point of being quite angry about something. I reminded him of his Buddha-nature and said, "Why don't you just be like the Buddha, and meditate as a way of breathing through these feelings?"

"Meditate?" he said, glaring at me. "Meditate?" Suddenly, he threw his hands into the air, and shouted, "I want to *kill!*"

I couldn't help but laugh. Here was my essentially peaceful, loving son, confessing that he was so angry he wanted to kill!

But his honesty cleared the energy, and his emotions came back into balance. He relaxed and actually chuckled at himself. We talked about what was bugging him, and suddenly it wasn't a big deal anymore.

I had to remind myself that Adam was also a normal kid who loved computers, video games, and action movies—and that with his Scorpio nature, he could be pretty intense at times.

His authenticity was just another indication to me that no matter how enlightened we are, no matter how transparent our ego, the ego always has its dark side. To be human is to cast a shadow. However, just as shadows disappear when the sun is overhead, so the more we stand in the bright light of truth and consciousness, the smaller our shadow will be. The more present and aware we are, the less likely we are to fall into unconscious behavior patterns. We see them as they arise, and we can refuse to give them power.

The person to be wary of is the one who smiles a little too plastically, and insists he or she never has an angry or violent thought. Understand this, accept your own flawed humanity with grace and humor, and your ego need not be a problem.

### NEGATIVE ENERGY

Negative energy is like a virus. It gets you in its grip, and it can be very hard to shake free. When you're really worried or obsessing about something, sometimes the best thing to do is just stretch, take a walk, and get involved in doing something until the tension lessens a bit.

If you want to be inwardly free, you have to face the issues that bother you over, and over, and over again. Daily meditation helps you do this. Learn to be with your anger, your fear, your confusion. Breathe into the energy. Surrender to it.

You can use your meditation time to really probe into the issues that are troubling you. After you've been sitting for long enough to feel reasonably clear and grounded (which should be no more than ten to fifteen minutes, once meditation becomes more natural for you), bring the issue or problem you want to explore into your awareness.

Look at it as you would any object. See the problem as a three-dimensional movie, or hologram—see the person involved, or the situation, or the particular circumstance. View it from the front and back, from both sides, and from the top and bottom. Then look deep inside it. Feel the energy behind it.

As you let your vision penetrate to the innermost core of the issue you're meditating on, it will gradually show itself to you. Like a knot, it will begin to unravel. Keep looking like this, keep bringing it into your meditation day after day if you need to, and there will come a moment when you see it with total clarity. You'll understand why you needed to struggle with it, and what the lesson was. Then it will dissolve and will no longer be a problem for you. You'll be free of it.

If ever your meditation becomes too intense, if it brings up uncomfortable emotions, feelings of restlessness, anxiety, fear, or disturbing energies or sensations in your body, you are always free to take a break. Come back to your sitting the next day. You'll feel stronger, and it will be easier to face and breathe through whatever it is that is demanding your attention.

When you deny negative feelings and emotions, they persist. If you allow them to fully reveal themselves in your awareness, they dissolve. Remember, it's the thoughts and images that keep the uncomfortable memories alive. When the intensity or negativity calms down a bit, that's the time to meditate. Just witness the thoughts that come up. Don't cling to them. Let them move through you. Gradually they will lose their hold over you.

Self-doubt, fear, and other negative emotions are normal as long as you continue to live from your ego, from identification with your personal "story." Until you fully realize the core insight and free yourself, the best way to deal with these negative states is not to give in to them. Stand firm and be present. Stay connected to the earth. Draw on the warrior energy within you. Face all your feelings and emotions, but don't let them overwhelm you.

Sometimes, during times of extreme grief, for example, the feelings may be just too intense. If this happens, there is nothing to do but be overwhelmed. Sometimes, for your healing, you may need to fall apart completely. Grief results from the loss of someone or something you've identified with—the ending of a love relationship, for example, or the death of a family member, or being laid off from what you thought was a secure job. It's healthy to mourn, to grieve such losses.

Understand what's happening at a deeper level, though. You're shedding a part of your old identity. You were defined, to some degree, by this person or situation. Ultimately, the letting go is bringing you closer to your true identity—who you are at the core of your very being. It's bringing you to the inner well-being that doesn't depend on outer circumstances, or mind-created identities.

It's hard to understand what is going on when you're in the middle of an intense emotional experience. The situation can be very confusing, especially if you've been abandoned or betrayed, or your heart has been broken. The understanding you so desperately seek won't come till later, after you've gone through the experience.

Trying to understand a process when you're in the middle of it only cuts you off from the experience—and the valuable learning to be had. Wait. Breathe. Be patient. The understanding will eventually come.

People rush to judge, to form conclusions too quickly. This tendency comes out of the mind's desperate need to "know," to be able to put a conceptual handle on things. As you learn to be more at ease in your body, more present in the moment, the need to "understand" will be less of a driving force.

Working through and releasing intense emotions and negative energy softens you, opens your heart. It brings you to a *real* understanding of what you've been going through, and why things happened as they did. You'll understand your part in the situation and the learning and growth to be had. (Tool #6, the Balancing Perceptions process, coming up shortly, will give you a step-by-step method for facilitating this.)

One of the quickest and most effective ways of shifting out of a headspace that doesn't feel good, such as worry, obsessive thinking, or some other form of mental conflict, is the following technique:

## TOOL #5
### STOPPING YOUR MIND

Meditation is usually about letting go of will, of making an effort, and being in a receptive mode. But for this exercise, you use your will—your ability to make something happen. You simply decide that for the next five, ten, or fifteen minutes, you're not going to think. You're not going to think about anything. You set your intention, make the commitment, and then you simply do it. For example, let's say you are taking a walk, or you're driving—or you can even experiment with it during your formal meditation period. You look at your watch, note the time, and then you simply get really present with your awareness.

Each time you observe yourself thinking, you just let the thoughts go—no matter what they are, whether they are positive or negative. (If you want to be free, you have to let go of everything.) The thoughts arise, you notice them, and you let them go. You come back to being very aware and alert in the present. You may think you cannot "wipe" thoughts away like this, but in fact it is quite easy to do. It just takes commitment and focus. You could certainly do it if you had a gun pointed to your head. Well, there *is* a gun pointed to your head! This is your mental, emotional, and spiritual well-being we are talking about here!

Usually, within a fairly short time of doing this exercise, something magical happens. The "glue"—the worrying "me"—that is causing the obsessive thoughts to recycle constantly through your head starts to dissolve. You no longer have to make an effort to release the individual thoughts. They just drop away, and suddenly it feels as if your head is poking through the clouds, and you experience a wonderful sense of freedom, of release. "Ah, what was all the fuss about?" you may find yourself sighing with relief.

I'll give you a personal example. Years ago I was dealing with a broken heart, the pain of a love affair that had ended in betrayal and deception. The woman I was in love with had left me for another man. For several months I obsessed over losing her, and tried everything I could to win her back. I was in such pain that I could not get her out of my mind.

One cold, wintry afternoon during this period, Adam wanted to go roller-skating, so we went to the local rink, which was crowded with the usual kids and a few brave adults. The music was loud as always, and it felt good to move. Adam was happy speeding around on his new Rollerblades and I did a reasonable job with my rented skates, but I couldn't get my ex-girlfriend out of my head.

Thinking about her was driving me crazy. I was so distracted that I narrowly missed running into other skaters, and I kept stumbling on the hard wooden floor. Then I remembered my Stopping Your Mind technique. I looked at my watch and decided that for the next fifteen minutes I would exercise my will and not think about her or anyone or anything. I would just get into the total experience of skating, the people, the loud music, the pale blue floor whizzing by beneath me.

What happened was a miracle. Within minutes my mind started to clear, and after about ten minutes I was in a totally different headspace. I felt connected to myself, to my deeper self, again. I felt free of her, and of all the pain of the past. As I continued to skate, I found I could even think of her and the thoughts no longer had any power to upset me. I was senior to them. I had transcended them. What a liberation!

That experience actually proved to be a major break-through, and the beginning of my true healing from the pain of that relationship. It allowed me to find myself again, to come back to the truth of my own being, independent of the hold she had previously exerted over me. It paved the way for the un-derstanding and embodiment of the core insight—that I was not my thoughts, my emotions, my circumstances. As you will see in chapter 4, which is about relationships, this ability to know and be oneself at all times, in all situations, is an essential key for personal happiness.

To release negative energy, then, focus less on the drama, the appearance, and more on the *dharma,* the inner truth. When life knocks you on your rear, try and think of it as hum-bling, rather than humiliating. You'll get back on your feet much quicker, and you'll learn from the experience.

Life has probably already shown you that there is definitely something to be learned through suffering. Look, then, for the lesson. Probe deeply. Eventually, you'll arrive at the question that, if you follow it all the way to the end, can liberate you from suffering altogether. That question is, Who is it that suffers?

In the meantime, be gentle and compassionate with your-self. Real wisdom is to be found in the heart.

## FREEDOM FROM BELIEFS

Beliefs make up a large part of the mind's content. Human be-ings have all kinds of beliefs about everything. But beliefs are not reality—and the more fully you live in reality, the less you need to "believe" anything.

It's human, however, to want to believe in something. Just don't be one of those people who seek something to believe in without ever questioning *why* they need to "believe" in the first place.

Beliefs can, however, serve a useful purpose. They help the mind operate with a degree of certainty. You may not yet have the *experience* of deep inner freedom and spiritual well-being, but believing in it as a possibility helps draw it to you. Beliefs, then, are a tool. They are *assumptions* about reality.

When you truly love someone or something, it has nothing to do with beliefs. You don't "believe" you love your child or your dog. You just *love* them. If you love someone based on what you "believe" to be so about them, your love is conditional and not true love at all. It's more like an infatuation. You're in love with an idea, an image, a projection.

The addiction to ideas and images is behind most human conflict. People who are overly identified with a particular belief system cause most of the problems in the world. They are always arguing and fighting with each other over their political, religious, or philosophical differences.

If you're emotionally attached to a belief—that your religion is the only true faith, that so-and-so is a good (or bad) person—then the opposite, or an alternate, possibility will throw you into conflict should it ever present itself. And you can be sure of one thing—contradictory beliefs sooner or later always do present themselves!

Your inner mental reality works on the principle of duality, pairs of opposites. You can't have the concept "black" without the idea of "white," just as you can't think "good" without having the notion "bad" somewhere in the back of your consciousness.

The mind thrives on duality, on naming objects, experiences, and events as "this" or "that." This is a necessary survival skill. It gives you the ability to discriminate between what supports your well-being and what threatens it.

Duality and naming things become a problem when there's an emotional attachment to the concepts. Being able to affix a name or label to a feeling, event, or thing may give the mind the feeling of certainty it seeks, but it's a false security.

As you get freer of your mind and live more from your heart, from your spiritual depths, you won't feel the same need to cling to beliefs and concepts for your identity. You'll use beliefs, but you won't rely on them to be at peace with yourself. Your sense of identity, of selfhood, will come from *being* itself—from being awake, alive, attuned to the vibrancy and fullness of the now moment.

Rigidly held beliefs tend to express themselves in muscular armoring, a lack of physical ease, grace, suppleness. In many fundamentalist religious groups, followers are taught not to trust their feelings, their inner experience, but to trust only the dogma being fed them. This can make a person feel very conflicted. There's a war going on between what they've been told and what they are actually feeling.

I worked with a woman once, Alice, who lived with this conflict to an extreme degree. It showed in her body. She was overweight, chronically tired, and was always in some kind of physical pain and discomfort. She had been raised in a religiously fundamentalist household. She had been married and divorced three times, because she was taught to believe that sex was only permissible in marriage; every time she was attracted enough to a man to want to have sex with him, she had to marry him.

The marriages themselves were disasters because neither she nor the men she married really knew themselves—and how can you be intimate and relate successfully to another when you don't have a deep intimacy with yourself?

Alice's main problem was that she simply didn't trust herself. She didn't trust her own inner wisdom. She was trying to break away from her fundamentalist past, and she would go to New Age and personal growth workshops where she would be advised to listen to her heart and trust her feelings. Immediately her past religious conditioning would come up and trigger self-doubt and guilt. She had been taught to place her faith in only one thing: the word of God, as it had been written down in the Bible and interpreted by her preachers. Never mind what she sensed or felt in the depths of her being.

Happily, Alice was gradually making the shift. She was letting go of her past programming with all its dogma and was discovering what we all, sooner or later, must learn: in order to get free of the addiction to beliefs, we must find out who we are—who this "I" is who so desperately needs to believe in something. Alice was beginning to develop a new and much more authentic relationship with God, with the power that created her—a relationship that depended less on other people's beliefs and more on what she felt and intuited in her own heart and soul.

When you find the security that doesn't depend on outer conditions, on creeds, scriptures, or formulas, you won't worry about what to believe. Observe young children, for example, how they play, explore, and enjoy the moment without having to rationalize or justify their actions in any way. They haven't yet learned to live in their minds, their egos. They are not analyzing, judging, or comparing their experience, so they don't feel anything missing. To young children, the experience of being alive is a delightful and ever-fascinating adventure. They still live very much from their hearts. That's their secret.

There's a current of divine energy, of goodness, that runs through all creation. As you connect with it and realize you *are* "it"—you are an expression of the divine—you'll see the futility of trying to find happiness through your mind, through knowledge, beliefs, fantasies. To discover this current is to taste the simple delight of just *being*. What a wondrous gift that is.

If you must believe in something, believe in your own innate worth and goodness—and that you *can* create the life you want. Give up your limiting beliefs and your need for a conceptual "handle" on life, and you'll start to experience the happiness that is your true, abiding nature.

## BALANCING PERCEPTIONS

The mind has to see its own limits. This is the value of intellectual clarity: it brings you to the indisputable realization that the freedom and happiness you seek can never be found through words and concepts.

When you are young, and if you are intellectually inclined, you get a lot of energy from dancing around in your mind, dissecting and constructing theories, speculating on the meaning of existence, playing with words and ideas. After doing it for ten, twenty, or thirty years, however, it starts to get old—especially if there is no underlying, body-based *experience* of peace, joy, well-being.

Seek truth, then. Find out who you are beyond your mind, beyond your mental and conceptual identity, beyond the psychological and emotional framework that has, up till now, governed your thoughts, behavior, and actions. Find out your *true* identity, who you are as a spiritual being. It's the surest way to arrive at genuine happiness, the happiness that does not depend on beliefs, other people, or the liquidity of your finances.

The final tool in this chapter is the Balancing Perceptions process, which I adapted from a technique developed by Dr. John Demartini, a chiropractor and inspirational speaker. What drew me to his approach was the realization that I had been, in my own way, using it throughout my life. Most of us do, in one form or another. It's about learning to look for the blessing in every difficult situation, for the gift in every problem. Here is the process as I use it in my work.

## TOOL #6
## BALANCING PERCEPTIONS

Choose a problem/issue in your life where you feel stuck or powerless to make a change. It could be in the area of health, relationships, emotions, work, spirituality, finances, or anything. Then take a sheet of paper and draw a vertical line down the middle of the page.

At the top of the page, write the problem, such as Why can't I find the right job? or How come I'm broke? Next, begin to take an inventory of all the negatives in the situation. This is the easy part! These are the beliefs, judgments, psychological/emotional tape loops that you've been playing over and over in your mind for months, years, often decades. It's the story you've been telling yourself for a long, long time.

To give you an actual example of the process, and one that is relevant to this chapter, let's say you have been struggling with making time for meditation. You sense the value of it but you can't seem to get around to doing it. You just begin to write down, line by line, everything that comes up for you around the subject. Here are three possible issues:

1. I feel uncomfortable in my body and experience pain when I sit.

2. I get bored and restless and find it impossible to get my mind to stop chattering.

3. I'm afraid if I meditate too much I'll become too passive, and then my outer life will start to fall apart.

Ideally, you should aim for ten to twenty negative beliefs or considerations about the problem you are exploring. Once you've written down the main issues that constitute your mind-set around the problem you're facing, pause to center and ground yourself. Be reflective. Now you are going to go down the other side of the column. You're going to take each consideration, one by one, and probe for the *positive,* for the blessing in it.

You're going to look for the gift in the situation—because in every negative, there is always a positive. It's just a matter of learning to shift your perspective. (You may find yourself unwilling, at first, to accept that there might be something positive in a negative, upsetting situation. But, I assure you, the positive is always there—and, once you begin to find it, you are already on the road to freedom.) Let's find the positives in the examples above. You might, after probing deeply into your own consciousness, find yourself coming up with the following:

1. This is showing me where I'm holding tension in my body, where I have difficulty relaxing and letting go. It's a sign that I need to become more conscious of my body, and of exercise. I may also benefit from getting some chiropractic or bodywork.

2. If nothing else, noticing how noisy and busy my mind is, is showing me how disconnected I've become from the clarity and inner peace that all spiritual teachings say is my true nature. I clearly need to stick with this meditation. (And maybe I need to review the way I'm approaching it. Maybe I could benefit from some instruction.)

3. I guess I have a lot of anxiety about stopping, being still, and letting go of control. Meditation will be an opportunity to face and work through my fears, and come to more balance in my life.

When you have balanced all the negatives with a positive, take a few minutes just to sit and *be* with what you have learned from this exercise. Then, as you go about your day (or go to bed that evening), remind yourself to do this one thing: every time you start to think negatively about *any* situation in your life, immediately counter the negative by saying to yourself, "Okay, so what's the blessing here? How is this serving me?"

Gradually, you will learn to instinctively balance your own perceptions of any situation. You won't even need to write them down. You'll do it automatically, within your own consciousness, and you won't get stuck in the negative again.

---

The Balancing Perceptions process is an amazingly simple, heart-centered approach to releasing stress, conflict, and self-doubt, and bringing you quickly to a place of clarity and unconditional love. It is based on a timeless spiritual truth: that emotional pain and suffering are the result of an imbalanced or lopsided perception. You believe or judge a particular event or circumstance to be negative, and it creates a painful emotional charge, or upset. (The fixed pattern of beliefs and judgments themselves were, typically, formed long ago, out of your childhood hurts and frustrations. They became part of your "story," your model of reality—the filters through which you tend to judge all your experience.)

However, it is a law of physics that for every negative, there is also a positive. This is a spiritual law as well. In every challenging situation, there is also a gift—the silver lining in the cloud. Problems are blessings in disguise.

By going through the Balancing Perceptions process above, what you find is that the positives and negatives eventually neutralize each other. They cancel each other out, and the emotional energy is discharged. You find yourself catapulted into an expanded awareness of the issue you've been exploring. It is now seen with clarity and insight.

You begin to understand that *all* beliefs and judgments, whether positive or negative, are ultimately just rationalizations, and that when you are truly free, you cling to neither the negative nor the positive but see things just as they are.

When you get the lesson, you "understand." You've literally figured it out, so that now you don't have to think about it anymore. In other words, it's no longer a problem—because problems, by definition, are situations that, real or imagined, require you to dwell on and think about them.

This clarity of seeing gives you a renewed sense of energy and personal power. The situation no longer runs you. You realize that you are bigger than it. Any action you need to take becomes obvious, and the courage necessary to take it springs forth on its own.

### THE TRUE NATURE OF MIND

As you get free of the limitations of thought, beliefs, judgments, and rationalizations, through awareness, meditation, and the Balancing Perceptions process, your mind itself will be liberated. You'll begin to intuitively grasp the true nature of your mind—that it is pure consciousness, multidimensional awareness, shot through with infinite powers of perception and creativity.

Quantum physics has demonstrated that the real nature of all phenomena is emptiness, electrons and particles dancing about in empty space. Emptiness is also your own real nature—but it's an emptiness that is rich in creative potential. The more you see this, the more your sense of "I" and "me" becomes transparent. You discover that when you keep your "I," your ego, out of your mind, and just let your mind do its own thing, something extraordinary happens. Your mind functions smoothly and flawlessly, a direct reflection of the marvelous intelligence behind creation—what some people might call the "Cosmic Mind."

The awakened mind sees the whole picture, and it sees with total clarity. It generates precise, laser-sharp thoughts and insights. It produces spontaneous flashes, brilliantly clear and imaginative pictures—and all just when you need them! In the body, you experience this multidimensional awareness as ease, openness, a lightness of being. In the heart, you experience it as joy, love, compassion.

Use the creative powers of your mind to your fullest capacity, but don't get so seduced by your own power to pursue some idealized future that you miss the beauty of the moment. Visualization and imagination are meant to enhance living, not substitute for it.

The mind doesn't choose. It just sees clearly and acts. It's the ego, the personal sense of "self," that chooses. If you want your mind to function optimally and allow you to fulfill your potential here, keep your "I," your ego, out of the thinking process.

Have you noticed how your life flows along just fine and everything feels beautifully balanced until "you" jump into the picture, and start worrying about things and trying to control them? The secret is to get out of your own way. Now, how many times in your life have you heard *that?*

Eventually, you get so attuned to your own thought processes that you learn there are certain paths of thought that are better not to go down. They only lead to negativity and despair, so why follow them?

I'll conclude this chapter with another story about Adam, because it highlights the power of meditation in bringing about a clear mind and awakening a deeper sense of well-being within.

This incident happened about six months after Adam "discovered" meditation during our hike in the hills. He had invited a friend over to stay. It was ten-thirty in the evening, and the two boys had gone to bed. I was at my Macintosh, writing. I heard the bedroom door open, and Adam came out, rubbing his eyes.

"I can't sleep, Dad," he said. "I feel restless. My mind's going all over the place. I need to meditate."

"Go ahead," I said, somewhat surprised, as he pulled out my *zafu,* my Zen meditation cushion.

I smiled as I watched him sit cross-legged on the cushion, with his hands resting on his knees and his eyes closed, just as he had seen me doing so many times. (I imagine if a man is an ardent golfer, then it is a precious moment for him when his son is old enough to finally pick up a golf club. It's no different for dads who have discovered the liberating joy of meditation!) Then I went back to my writing.

Some time later, I heard Adam making a few happy gurgling sounds, and sighing in a contented way. I glanced over at him. His eyes were still closed. He sighed again, and said out loud, "Ah, that's better, I can feel my own energy again. I think I'll sit here for a few minutes more."

He sat for perhaps five more minutes, then got up and came over to me and said, "I feel great now. Thanks, Dad." He hugged me, gave me a kiss on the cheek, told me he loved me, and then went to bed.

I sat there in wonder—even, a little, in awe. If I've done nothing else for my son in eleven years, I thought to myself, but teach him how to reconnect with his own energy whenever he feels fragmented and distracted, I've given him a pretty important gift.

How many adults in our culture, whenever they feel stressed or out-of-sorts, have the knowledge to do what Adam did, I thought? To find their own center, the true ground of their being, through the practice of meditation? Too many too often resort to food, alcohol, drugs, or TV to numb out their overstimulated or overactive minds. I'd been similarly addicted myself, before I discovered the power of meditation. What a blessing, to know how to reconnect with oneself in this way.

The good news is that meditation itself starts to happen more effortlessly as you open your heart and connect with your essense, your true spiritual nature—and the more you live from your essence, the more everything else in your life starts to fall into place.

In the next chapter, we'll explore in more depth the art of opening to spirit.

CHAPTER THREE

# Opening to Spirit

## THE REALITY OF SPIRIT

*T*he spiritual dimension in life is more real than any of the physical things you see. Every "thing" created, from rocks to trees to animals to human beings, sooner or later disappears, but spirit is forever. It is timeless, eternal. When you really understand this, when you actually begin to feel spirit's healing presence in your body, mind, and heart, it frees you from fear, loneliness, and self-doubt.

The happiest people have discovered that while good fortune in the outer world is always a blessing—and a necessary element for a whole and balanced life—true happiness comes from within. Such people have learned the wisdom of making their spiritual well-being their first priority. Their primary joy comes from being filled and enlivened with that inexhaustible current of life energy we call *spirit*.

What is spirit? It is the fundamental creative energy of life. Your "spirit" is that energy as it expresses through *you*. Some people refer to this personal manifestation of spirit—the non-material, essential self—as "soul." As always, what matters more than the names and distinctions is the experience of peace, oneness, harmony.

Spirit is an energy you can actually experience in your body as ease and fullness, in your mind as clarity and insight, and in your heart as love and joy. Meditation, the art of consciously being quiet and still and tuning in to the subtle presence that underlies creation, is the most direct way to connect with the energy of spirit.

Meister Eckhart, the fourteenth-century German mystic, said, "The less there is of 'I,' the more there is of God." Spirit works its miracles in your life only to the degree that you're open to it, that you invite it in. Otherwise, you're living from your personal sense of "self," from your ego, with all its doubts, insecurities, fears.

When you live from your ego, you literally shut the higher power out. You close the door to God. Spiritual awakening is getting free of attachment to your personal "self" and opening up to your true Self, your God-nature.

Spirit is the source of all beauty. We love beauty in all its forms precisely because it reconnects us with spirit. Think about that the next time you admire someone or something beautiful, or when you're out enjoying the beauty of nature.

This is why it is important to have beauty in your life. Not just the surface beauty associated with good looks and a great image, but the beauty that has depth and soul to it. A beautiful environment, beautiful art, beautiful music, a beautiful, heart-felt connection with your friends.

Beauty is that which evokes the feeling of perfect harmony, or balance. Beauty is love made visible. Beauty heals. And spirit is the energy behind it all.

### SPIRIT AND RELIGION

There's a difference between spirit and religion. Spirit is the life force, the essential impulse behind all creation. Religion, in its highest form, is an organized effort to understand, codify, and share the healing and redemptive power of spirit.

If you look into the heart of all authentic spiritual traditions, both of the East and the West, you'll find the same message being said over and over again: the treasure you seek most is to be found within the depths of your very own being.

Jesus taught this when he said the kingdom of heaven is within you. First find the riches within, he stated, and then the worldly things you need will come to you. This is the timeless, spiritual way to a happy and balanced life.

The Buddha taught that suffering is the result of ignorance, and that enlightenment—wisdom and bliss—is your natural state. The Hindu Upanishads say "You are *That*"—you are a manifestation of the divine, the One power behind all reality. The Islamic Sufis teach that when you strip away the veils of ego, of personal "self," what is left is God in human form. The Tao Te Ching tells us that when your mind and heart open to the deeper flow of reality, the whole world belongs to you. Mastery of being leads to effortless doing, and there is nothing that can't be accomplished.

The more you awaken to your spirituality, the less you'll need to hold tightly to any kind of formal religious belief or practice. Religion is based on beliefs; spirituality, on *experience*. Religion is the story, spirituality is what the story is about.

Most religions tell a truly amazing story about God and creation, but they are still stories. Whether you choose to believe in them or not is up to you. Beliefs are of the mind, the head. Faith is of the heart. The more you open to your own direct spiritual experience, independent of any story, the more your faith in the innate beauty and goodness of life deepens. Then your religion, whatever it is, will have more richness and meaning for you.

In almost all cases, people who go through a near-death

experience notice a shift in their relationship to religion, to the metaphysical or cosmological "story." Having experienced first-hand their connection to God, or whatever you want to call the mystery and power behind creation, a formalized system of beliefs becomes unnecessary. Once you *know* that you are one with creation, and that there is really nothing to fear, you don't need to espouse or cling to any beliefs about the matter. What a marvelous freedom that is!

Most organized religions insist you need an agent—a church, a priest, a holy book, a savior—in order to know God. Sometimes, this insistence comes from a well-intentioned place, but all too often it's motivated by a desire to control your experience. Think about this the next time some religious "authority" condemns you or tries to make you feel guilty or unworthy in some way.

That's why it is always important, as the bumper sticker says, to question authority. That way you can be the author of your experience, rather than having some other "authority" define reality for you.

Truth needs no agent. The quickening force behind creation that is spirit can only be experienced in the individual human heart and soul. As you awaken to the truth of your being, you may still honor a particular religious tradition, but you won't be bound by it.

You may still worship as a Christian, a Moslem, a Buddhist, a Jew, or something else, but you will not let the religious rituals, scriptures, or practices blind you to your true nature and the ultimate oneness of all creation. You'll nod your head in understanding when you hear the Dalai Lama say, as he did, "My religion is compassion and kindness."

As you open up spiritually, beliefs about the meaning of life will become less relevant. You'll know the truth in the core of your being, and what you know will not hinge upon words or concepts. That is why Lao Tzu wrote, "He who knows does not say, he who says does not know." The more connected you are to the truth of spirit, the more you realize it can't be talked about (though you may certainly use words to point to it). The less connected you are, the more you grasp at words and beliefs as a substitute for the experience.

When you cling rigidly to beliefs of any kind you become inflexible, constricted—even, in the extreme, irrational. Conflict and disharmony will follow you like a shadow. Holding your beliefs lightly, but with affection, is the sign of an open, flexible, sensitive personality. There is room for growth, new learning, spontaneity, responsiveness. This is the path of balance.

In the end, you can only *be* it. You're either being it—a kind, loving, and authentic person—or you're not. If you still have burning questions about religion and its place in your life, think for a moment about the root meaning of the word. It comes from the Latin *re-ligare,* "to tie, or fasten." To me, that means religion is about getting connected. It's about making the connection to spirit, your deeper Self, who you are beyond all your ideas and beliefs about who you are.

Behind all religious movements is a genuine impulse for good, for truth. The prophets of old were wise and compassionate men and women who were motivated by a vision of wholeness and balance—by their desire to unite humanity under one divine principle.

As we enter the new millennium, as each of us awakens to our true spiritual nature, one thing becomes very clear: regardless of the particular form of religious worship we may prefer, we, humanity, will come together only when everyone practices the religion of the heart.

## INTERCONNECTEDNESS

Modern quantum physics is discovering what the Buddha woke up to 2,500 years ago—that reality is an infinite field of energy and consciousness. We live in a holographic universe, where each part contains the whole, just as each individual drop of seawater contains the essence of the ocean. The universe, in other words, is God. Or, if you prefer, God is the universe unfolding. God is the whole thing.

Once I was at a talk given by Jean Klein. A woman stood up and asked him what he thought about God.

"God is a concept," Jean replied.

You could feel the silence. God is a concept. It sounded so heretical, yet everyone knew it was somehow true. "God" was the word humanity had come up with to describe whatever the incredible intelligence or mystery or force was that had created all of this. The word was so charged. We, humanity, had made "God" into this awesome entity that had the power of life, death, and eternal judgment over us.

Because of the conflicts that existed within me when I was young, I formed a close personal relationship with God. I envisaged him as this great, kindly old man who lived up in the sky, and who watched over me. I used to pray all the time. I loved God. He was a very real and constant presence in my life.

As I got older and more in touch with my own power, my need for God began to lessen. Prayer became more intermittent. Once I began getting into meditation and actually having deep and prolonged experiences of oneness, of connectedness with the spiritual energy that drives creation, I found it harder and harder to believe in some conceptual idea of "God."

One evening, I was lying in bed, grappling with some emotional turmoil. I decided to pray, something I hadn't done in a long time. "Dear Lord . . . ," I began, but then I stopped. The thought arose in my mind: "Jim, just who or what do you think you're praying to? Do you really think God is separate from you?"

As I got very still, very present, and became aware of the energy within and around me, my mind cleared, and peace suddenly prevailed once again. I realized that, for me, the idea of "God" as some separate force or energy *apart* from me was inconceivable.

"We are God" was the thought that passed through my mind. "We are all, each one of us, expressions of the divine."

That was the last time I ever prayed in that way. Every so often, I find myself spontaneously offering a prayer of thanks to the universe, to that source energy of which I am a manifestation. Of which we are all manifestations. Indeed, the more we wake up to the true nature of existence, the more gratitude—as I said in the introduction to this book—becomes our daily prayer.

The ocean metaphor is a good way to facilitate the deepening of your connection to spirit, the divine. David Bohm, a physicist who was both a protégé of Albert Einstein and a friend and colleague of J. Krishnamurti, the renowned spiritual teacher, once commented on the energy potential in the universe. "In one cubic centimeter of empty space," he said, "there is the energy equivalent of twenty kilotons of TNT."

The space around you, then, is filled with energy, and because consciousness has no borders, because you can extend your awareness out to an infinite degree, it is not too much of a stretch to think of yourself as living in an ocean of energy and consciousness. And if the space around you is the ocean, then "you" are like a wave on the ocean.

As a wave, you are an expression of the ultimate energy. Just like a wave, you have your own unique individuality, your own style, character, and temperament. This is your personality in this lifetime. The more awake you are to your essential spiritual nature—the ocean—the less attached you are to your "wave-ness." You honor your individuality, but you don't become infatuated with it.

People get scared, anxious, and lonely because they know themselves only as "waves." They look at the world out there, all the other "waves," and it feels like a very competitive, hostile, and threatening environment.

Discover your connection to the ocean, the ground of Being, and you'll no longer feel separate or alienated. You'll experience, at the deepest level, the interconnectedness—the exquisite balance—of all life. The following exercise will allow you to taste this firsthand—and, as the great Sufi poet Rumi said, to taste is to know. This really works well if you have a friend read it to you:

## TOOL #7
## INTERCONNECTEDNESS

Sit with your back straight, keep your eyes open, pay attention to your environment. Drink in your surroundings through your eyes. Really connect with what you see. Then take a few deep breaths, close your eyes, and bounce your shoulders up and down a few times to release any tension in them. What you're going to do now is to start visualizing the space between your joints.

Begin with your ankles. Visualize them internally, especially the space between the surfaces of the bones. See if you can actually feel the space. Feel it as a kind of openness in the joint. Then bring your attention to your knees and do the same thing. Pause awhile as you feel the space behind your kneecap and between your thigh bone and your tibia, the lower leg bone. Once you get a sense of this, move up to your hip joints. Feel one side, then the other. Pay attention to the thin space between the ball and socket. Now move your awareness slowly up your spine, one vertebra at a time. Notice the discs that separate each vertebra, feel their spongy softness. When you get to your neck, move out to the shoulder joints and feel the space there, where the upper arm connects to the scapula. Let your awareness expand so that you can visualize both shoulders simultaneously.

Then let your inner eye travel down to the elbows. Linger awhile there, then move your attention down to the bones in both wrists and the joints between your fingers. At each point you stop, you are visualizing and feeling space, openness, lightness. Lastly, on this phase of your internal journey, curl your hands slightly and feel the hollowness in your palms. Feel the energy that radiates from them. When you've completed this, bring your awareness back to your neck and slowly travel up to where the topmost vertebra joins your skull. Feel the space here. Feel how your head sits lightly but firmly atop your spine. Then visualize the space inside your mouth, the cavity behind your cheeks. Let your mouth and jaw relax so that the space inside your mouth can expand.

Now take about fifteen or twenty seconds to scan your entire body from head to toe and back again, feeling the sense of expansion, of spaciousness and ease, inside you. Feel that spaciousness as pure energy. Feel your true, inner nature as luminous energy—clear, still, vibrant. At the same time, start paying attention to the energy outside your body, the energy of your environment. Notice if the energy in the air around you is different than the quality of the energy you feel inside.

Then visualize the pores of your skin opening and expanding, so that your internal energy can move outwards. Feel the pores of your skin growing larger and larger, until your skin itself becomes almost transparent, a gossamer web lightly containing the luminous energy that is your true nature. Let your inner energy merge with the energy around you. Be very still as you do this. Notice how the two en-

ergies merge and become one. The inner and outer are not different. There is only one energy.

Feel the ocean of energy that is your true nature. Feel how your
body is like a wave dancing lightly on the ocean. Then open your
eyes. Consciously feel your connection, your oneness, with the underlying flow, the current, of life and creation.

---

There is only one energy, but it manifests in an infinite mul-
tiplicity of forms. You are one of the forms, as is every other human being, every living and nonliving thing. You are a unique,
individualized expression of the source energy.

As the truth of interconnectedness becomes more real for
you, you'll think twice about causing harm to any other person
or thing. You'll have more respect for all forms of life. You'll feel
their suffering as if it were your own. This is how spirituality
gives rise to compassion, to love.

As your compassion grows, it'll be hard for you to even
squash a bug. You'd rather trap a spider and release it outdoors
than hurt it. At the same time, if you're being attacked by a
mosquito, don't feel guilty if you swat it in self-defense. It's
okay to protect yourself.

The spiritual journey is about finding the connection
within. It is about coming home, discovering that your true
home is within you, in the heart. Think of a child, a small boy,
wandering out in the woods, away from home. He feels safe and
loved because the feeling and memory of "home" are still
freshly with him. But if he wanders too far and gets lost, then
he panics. He no longer remembers where home is.

Spiritual paths are like maps for the journey home. They
guide you back to the source, to the wholeness that is your true
nature. But once you know where home is, once you know how

to get back, even in the most difficult of times or circumstances, then you can put the maps aside. Then a spiritual "path," with its practices and techniques, becomes unnecessary—except when you forget!

When you're awake spiritually, you're always at home—or never far from it—no matter where you are. This is why spiritual work is so important in finding balance in the world. As you awaken to the core insight and find out who you are beyond your personal history, you start to experience a constant flow of ease, of inner joy and well-being, and it is this that guides you safely and smoothly through the ups and downs of daily existence.

The work is to get your ego, your personal will out of the way, and allow something bigger to move through you. Then your personal will becomes aligned with divine will, and your actions benefit everyone they touch.

### FREEDOM FROM THE FEAR OF DEATH

Change no longer frightens you, because you realize that while every "thing" sooner or later changes, spirit—which is not a "thing" but is, rather, the very source of all "things"—is constant. The constancy of spirit, its timelessness, nourishes and sustains you through all of life's difficulties and challenges. Spirit itself becomes the pivotal energy that keeps your life in balance.

The realization that one day your body is going to die doesn't scare you any longer, either. When you really feel your connection to the ocean of energy, the larger "ground" of Being, you just know, in your heart, that it's all okay. Dying, like birth itself, is but a transition from one realm to another. Your soul is on an endless journey through an endless number of realms. This is one way of looking at the mystery of life and death.

For these *are* the two great mysteries, aren't they? The mystery of birth and of death? Different religions offer explanations for them. They attempt to take the fear out of dying by promising a heaven, an afterlife, or something else of that sort.

However, the more you know yourself as a spiritual being, the less you need the explanations. You'd rather just be present and discover the mystery of birth and death for yourself. This is why it is such a gift to be present at the birth of a child, whether it's your own or someone else's. Or to be present at the bedside of someone who is dying, to hold their hand, to look lovingly into their eyes, to feel them letting go. Ah, such grace, such wonder, such mystery!

When you're awake spiritually, you learn to face each moment consciously, to trust the deeper wisdom of life. You'll face the moment of death in the same way. This is the true warrior's aim: to live and die consciously—for as you've lived, so will you die. Live courageously, and you will not be afraid of death.

To breathe your last in this life is to breathe your first in the next. If you're at peace with yourself, you don't even think about dying anyway. You're too engaged here in the present. Thoughts about the "past" and the "future" no longer distract you from what is real *now*.

Now, now, now. One step at a time. Learn to stay in the present, totally in the present, and all fear will gradually leave you. In a very real sense, you're learning to die each moment. "Die to the past," Krishnamurti used to say. Let go of your psychological and emotional holding, your attachment to "I," "me," and "mine," and you'll be born anew in the present. Again, and again, and again.

Live in your ego-based worries and concerns and you forget God, you forget the Source, your true nature. Then fear is always looking over your shoulder. You'll take that fear with you, even into death.

Dr. Elisabeth Kubler-Ross tells about a little boy who was dying and who said death is like walking into your mind. Ah, out of the mouths of babes! Such wisdom from such a young soul. To die so young, but what a gift that little boy has given us. If your mind is cluttered with fear, judgments, and conflict when you approach your death, walking into your mind isn't going to be very pleasant at all. In fact, certain religions have a name for the experience. They call it Hell.

This is why it's so important to do inner work. It's the only way you can get clear. Pursue spiritual knowledge, meditate, pray, know yourself, work on releasing all the "stuff" that weighs so heavily, at times, on your mind and heart. Then death won't be so scary. In fact, the clearer you get, the more fear will leave you altogether. Then, when you die, you'll walk into a mind filled with light, peace, love. . . . And that, if you haven't already figured it out, is Heaven!

When I traveled to India many years ago as part of my spiritual quest, I made a pilgrimage to Rishikesh, a small town by the Ganges in the foothills of the Himalayas. There were a lot of yoga ashrams there, and I thought it would be a good place for retreat. One morning I went down to the small bazaar for *chai,* hot, sweet, and spicy Indian tea.

As I got my small clay cup of *chai,* I noticed there was one other Westerner among the crowd of customers. He stood out. He was tall, handsome, had long black hair and a beard streaked with gray, and he was dressed in a white robe.

I introduced myself. His name was Erhard. He was a German and ran a yoga ashram in Encinitas, California. He came to Rishikesh every year for advanced meditation study with his guru.

As we talked, it became clear to me that Erhard, who was maybe ten years older than me, was in a place in his consciousness where I longed to be myself. He seemed remarkably free and open. I remember looking at him and asking, with typical Sagittarian forthrightness, "Do you mean to say you know who you are?"

He returned my gaze without blinking. He actually smiled. "Yes," he said, "I do. But then, my quest for truth began early. I was a child living in Dresden at the end of the war when the Allies began their carpet-bombing raids. It was a terrifying time. I got to face my fear of death very early on."

I haven't seen Erhard since that one meeting, but I've always remembered him—his presence, and his confidence. What he had accomplished was what I longed for myself. I, too, wanted to be able to say that I knew who I was. I wanted that kind of inner certainty of being.

A powerful dream I had around the same time played a major role in freeing me from the fear of death, and brought me closer to true self-knowing. In the dream I found myself in a time tunnel. I was being pulled back, at incredible speed, through what appeared to be all my past lives, my previous incarnations, until I suddenly found myself stopped at the very first incarnation I ever experienced.

It was in prehistoric times and I was some kind of a large, lizardlike creature, sitting motionless on a rock, head craned forward, looking out at the savannah below me, where dinosaurs roamed. And what I became aware of was that the consciousness that looked through those lizard eyes was the same consciousness that looked through the eyes of all the subsequent incarnations, animal and human . . . and was the same consciousness that looked through the eyes of the person I was now, the dreamer.

In the dream, as I found myself once more in the reality of this, my current incarnation, the phrase "I am the Ancient One" sounded in my head. I knew then that my real nature was consciousness, and that as consciousness, I was simply incarnating, or manifesting, in an endless variety of forms. The forms are born and they die, but consciousness just *is*.

This is what brings freedom from the fear of death—the awakening to the truth of being, to your true nature as consciousness, as the timeless awareness behind all phenomena.

You can actually get a direct experience of this for yourself. The next time you're with someone you trust, look deeply into their eyes and imagine, or visualize, that the consciousness looking through their eyes at you is the *same* consciousness looking through your eyes at them. Play with this process often enough (doing it with your lover really gives you a taste of it), and one day you'll experience that there is, indeed, only *one* consciousness, shining through an infinite number of pairs of eyes. It's an awesome realization!

Ponder this idea. Meditate on it. Remember it the very next time you look into someone's eyes. Be very aware that they are truly just a reflection of you. If you see darkness, fear, and judgment, it's because you know these things in yourself. If you see beauty, love, and light, it's because these are in you. Look beyond the fear, see the light.

When you free yourself from the story, from the rigid identification with "I" and "me," you come to the realization that in fact nobody is born and nobody dies. You, as a historical person, exist only as an idea, a concept, inside your head.

Your body is born, yes, but you are not your body. You are much much more. When your body dies, "you" simply dissolve back into the ocean of consciousness that is your true nature. And then, as consciousness, if you want to be born into a body so that you can play in the world again—so that you can contribute, help out—you will! Consciousness is *always* waking up somewhere in some "form," some "body." The dream I just shared with you showed me that beyond any doubt.

The following lines, from the fifteenth-century Sufi poet Kabir, in a version by Robert Bly, say it exquisitely:

> *The idea that the soul will join with the ecstatic*
> *just because the body is rotten—*
> *that is all fantasy,*
> *What is found now is found then.*
> *If you find nothing now,*
> *you will simply end up with an apartment in the City of Death.*
> *If you make love with the divine now,*
> *in the next life you will have the face of satisfied desire.*

No matter where you go, there you are. No matter what reality you find yourself in, you, as consciousness, are always present. Stay conscious, die to the past, be present now, and the mystery of the body's dying will no longer hold any real fear for you.

## SPIRITUALITY IS IN THE HEART

Seek enlightenment, self-knowledge, spiritual freedom. It's the most important work you can do, both for your own healing and for that of the planet. It is what will help bring our world into balance.

Don't confuse enlightenment with sainthood. This is where so many people get hung up on enlightenment, and why they think it's so far out of reach. They think that being enlightened means you have to be some kind of saint, that you somehow have to be "above" all the normal human pleasures and indulgences. That's just not true.

Realizing your true spiritual nature, which is what enlightenment is, is absolutely attainable. It's within reach of everyone. Indeed, it's your birthright. You just have to want it badly enough, get clear about what it is and is not, and then do the inner work necessary to wake up to it.

Saints, by definition, are people of exceptional holiness and purity. They have let go of the normal human needs for security, pleasure, sex, and material possessions. They have given their lives over to the selfless service of humanity.

Most of us are not destined or even meant to be saints. We are here to enjoy all that life has to offer, but in a spiritually conscious, sensitive, and compassionate way. That's what the lesson of balance is all about. In any case, sainthood is something that is conferred upon a few rare individuals in any era—like a Mother Teresa, for example. And you can be sure of one thing: as long as you "hope" to be a saint, you'll never make it!

When your focus is just on getting enlightened, on the other hand, you still get to enjoy and satisfy all your human needs and desires. You can still enjoy drinking wine, making love, earning money, and pursuing the goals that matter to you.

Part of the deal, however (if you *really* want enlightenment), is that you can't be attached to these things. You can play hard in the game of life, and you can play to win, but you must not be attached to the outcome, the final result. That's what it means to be enlightened. You're not holding on to anything inside. You're inwardly free. Your heart is wide open, and you're already at peace. Your happiness doesn't depend on whether you win or lose at the outer game. You've already won the big prize!

An ancient Buddhist teaching says, "Let those who desire enlightenment not train in many practices, but only one. Which one? Great compassion. Those with great compassion possess all the Buddha's teaching as if it were in the palm of their hand."

The mind creates the universe through thinking and visioning, but the heart is the pump that nurtures creation and allows it to flourish. The mind can create extraordinary things. Modern technology is evidence of that. But without the heart's affection, caring, and love, what the mind has created sooner or later withers and dies.

To understand all this, and to live it, is the essence of the way of harmony.

## FEELING THE ENERGY OF SPIRIT

Spirit is the name we give to the source energy, to divine Being, to God. There are many ways to connect with the energy of spirit—meditation, prayer, walking in nature, gardening, making love, playing with your children, doing any task contemplatively, with full attention in the moment. The main thing is that you connect.

Find an activity that gets you in tune with spirit, and make *that* your spiritual practice. Make it conscious, however. Realize why you're doing it. Then your practice will work for you with increasing ease and consistency.

To discover your true spiritual nature, you must learn to be alone. First, you have to learn to be alone with your thoughts. Then you have to learn to be alone without thoughts. You have to let go of your attachment to thinking so that you can open up to silence and stillness, for it is here that you touch and feel the beauty of spirit.

Sitting in silence and being totally attuned to the present moment, to the underlying movement of spirit, is the shortest and most direct way home. To be present like this is to open yourself up to the energy, to feel it in every cell of your body.

You can talk about spiritual matters all you want, but there's no substitute for contact time with the energy. Concepts and theories feed the mind, but they don't satisfy the heart. For that, you need to actually *feel* the energy we call "spirit."

Feeling the energy of spirit is sometimes made easier if you first see clearly and are able to tune in, at a visual level, to the underlying wholeness and connectedness of all phenomena. This next tool is an extension of the previous one and will help facilitate the connection:

## TOOL #8
## VISUALIZING SPACE

You remember the Expanding Awareness exercise, where you see and feel yourself as the space in which your body appears, in which breathing happens, in which thoughts, feelings, and sensations come and go. You are now going to enlarge upon, or extend, this capacity for visualizing the space, or awareness, that is your true nature.

Begin by holding your hand out in front of you with your fingers spread out. Notice your hand and fingers and then focus on the background, the space around your hand and between your fingers. (It is like looking at a line drawing on white paper, and then shifting your gaze to the white background of the paper itself.) Then extend your gaze out farther to an object in front of you. If you are indoors, it may be a vase, a flower, a piece of furniture, or this book; if outdoors, a tree, a building, a wall, or fence-post. You can also make the object of your attention a person. Focus on the object, and then expand your focus to the space *around* the object.

Now follow the space around the object to the object nearest it, and then the one next to that. Get a sense of how this space, this openness, is the background to every "thing"—that every object that can be perceived has its existence within this infinite field of space or emptiness.

As you do this exercise, remind yourself that this "empty" space in which objects appear is actually an ocean of energy. Some people with heightened psychic ability can even "see" the energy. They may see a shimmering brightness, an aura, around the object. Sometimes there will even be colors. They may perceive the larger space between and behind objects as an invisible web of energy strands, the matrix that gives rise to and supports all physical phenomena. (If you want to "see" energy in this way yourself, simply set your intention, begin to look for it, and be open to what happens.)

Practice this way of seeing periodically throughout the day until you become familiar with it. You're teaching yourself to become familiar with the background to individual objects, the common spiritual/energetic source out of which all objects arise. It will help you see the "whole," the big picture. You'll be less caught up in and distracted by individual events and circumstances. You'll feel even more deeply the fundamental interconnectedness, the underlying unity and flow, of life.

---

It's important to notice what distracts you from being present, from feeling the connection to spirit. The world, with its endless temptations and diversions—money, sex, entertainment, power, success—is a very seductive place. Something catches your eye—a beautiful woman, a handsome man, a big house, an exotic car—and you end up looking away from the one place where what you *really* want is to be found.

There's absolutely nothing wrong with pursuing your worldly dreams and desires, but if you allow yourself to get so swallowed up by them that you lose yourself in the process, you'll never truly be happy. In fact, the farther you stray from the truth in your heart and soul, the truth of your being, the more miserable you'll be. That's pretty much a law of life. Call it the prime spiritual law.

Spirit is the "hum," the heartbeat of the universe. It is the ceaseless vibration behind creation, the intelligence that holds it all together in perfect cosmic symmetry. The bliss and joy of spirit dissolves all problems, all conflicts. When you connect with it, you find yourself at peace, happy, content just to *be*. You need or want for nothing.

The beauty of spirit is that it doesn't cost a single penny, though you do have to give up something. You have to give up all your mental ideas and concepts, your desire to become someone or something. You have to be empty, still, open. Then, soon, you'll hear the whisper of spirit.

Learn to tap into the energy of spirit, the tangible presence behind existence, and you'll have discovered life's greatest gift. Then you can move in the world as the beautiful person you really are. Then you can create a life that is a magnificent expression of *you*.

You'll be guided by spirit at every turn.

## NATURE AS HEALER

There is an underlying order, balance, and harmony in nature that, when you open to it, can heal and transform you at the very deepest level. Even in its storms, its cataclysms, its times of upheaval it can be cleansing, as in the sparkling clarity and freshness that follow a heavy rainfall.

Nature brings you back to yourself, to something pure and essential within you. It brings you back to your spiritual source. To spend time in nature is to return to your beginnings, your original state. It is to be renewed in body, mind, and soul.

Your body is your link to the natural world, because your body is of nature. It is of the earth. This is why a heightened body awareness is so critical to balance, to true well-being. You nurture your body, and thus your soul, the spiritual "you" that inhabits your body, every time you return to nature's embrace.

Taking a walk in the hills, strolling along the seashore, going into the woods, working in a garden, feeling your bare feet on the soft grass, or spending time with animals are all ways of reconnecting with nature. To come back to nature is to counterbalance the stressful effects of constant busyness and other man-made preoccupations. "Nature is the true teacher of Zen," said Suzuki Roshi, the Zen master who founded the San Francisco Zen Center.

Notice how when you climb up to a peak or promontory and look back down on the terrain from whence you came, you get perspective on life. Problems don't seem as important. This is how nature heals. Her energy is so vast, so timeless, so perfect a manifestation of harmony and balance that your own personal problems cannot sustain themselves.

It would be as if you were to let a drop of black ink fall into a large, crystal-clear pond. The drop would simply disappear. It would dissolve into the larger clarity of the pond. In fact it is the pond that cleanses and transforms the ink, taking it back into its own, returning it to its source.

So it is with nature, and one of the wisest moves you can make whenever you feel confused, upset, or conflicted in some way is to get outdoors and reconnect with nature. It's what I always used to do whenever I needed insight or healing. I'd take a hike up in Annadel, the lovely state park behind the city of Santa Rosa, not far from where I lived.

Within an hour of starting on the hike, I'd be completely absorbed in the beauty of the park, the silence, the spiritual energy that I'd feel there, and all my problems would just fall away. I'd feel connected to my true Self again. I'd feel one with that energy, that power we call God. And by the time I started back home, I'd have much more clarity about what action I needed to take, if any, with the issues or problems that had been bothering me so much.

In nature you get a direct experience of the mystery and power behind existence. Nature reminds you that spirit is always here, that the energy of creation is an actual, palpable reality. You feel it in the breath of the wind, in the chirping of a bird, in the hum of insects, and in the extraordinary silence beneath it all.

During the journey to India that I mentioned a few pages back, I was accompanied by my girlfriend. We were spending time in Nepal and had signed up for a three-day rafting trip on the Trisuli River with a dozen other Westerners. With our guides, we were eight people in each of two inflatable rafts.

On the second afternoon, we went down some very strong rapids. They seemed to go on forever. The raft was tossed about violently, and it took everything we had to not be thrown overboard. Finally, we shot out into a wide expanse of totally calm river. There were high cliffs to the right of us and a low embankment and beach to the left.

The raft glided almost to a stop, and the noise of the rapids faded. Everything became quiet, utterly still. No one spoke. There was just silence, a profound spiritual presence. You could feel the energy of the entire universe in that moment, the birth of creation itself right there on that river, in the foothills of the Himalayas.

My girlfriend and I looked at each other. We breathed at the same time, and breathed again. The energy was exquisite, almost overpowering. And then, before we could take a third breath, everyone else on the raft suddenly started chattering. It was as if the silence had become too much for them, so deep and vast was it.

We gave each other a nod of acknowledgment, grateful for the gift we had just received. We had come to the Himalayas on a spiritual journey. We had come to these mountains at the top of the world to go deeper into spirit, and we had been shown, once again, that in the silence underneath the sounds and noises of nature and life, spirit in all its purity and immensity was always there.

The others in the raft had a different agenda, perhaps. Maybe they had come to Nepal for other reasons. For so many people, such deep silence is still something that is a little scary, a space that must be filled at any cost. Before you can truly appreciate and love the beauty and power of silence, you have to open yourself to it. You have to be willing to leave the internal noise and dialogue behind. It is really about trusting the unknown.

The gift of nature is that she teaches you to trust. She insists you relate to her in the present. In nature, none of your ideas or theories make any difference. In the immensity and silence of nature, you begin to find silence and space within yourself.

You feel your body in a new way. You reconnect not only with your spiritual essence but also with your physical animal-nature. You begin to experience yourself at the level of pure *being,* without concepts, words, identities. You feel a sense of wholeness, oneness, and inner balance that erases all your doubts and questions about spirituality, religion, and the meaning of life.

## WALKING IN THE WORLD WITH BALANCE

Because the energy of spirit is so tremendously healing, it's tempting to get attached to it, to become so addicted to bliss or rapture that you neglect your other responsibilities in life. This is how people with really strong spiritual inclinations can get out of balance.

Altered states can be very seductive, but just because you've learned, through meditation and detachment, to transcend your problems, it doesn't mean they go away. When you come back to earth, the problems are still there—often more pressing than ever. Make sure you don't fall into the transcendence trap!

You may touch the source of spiritual energy, but if you fail to embody it, to find it in your relationships, your work, your business dealings, your everyday life, you'll lose it again.

Some spiritual traditions talk about the need to deny or transcend the body. This often springs from a fear of the sensual, and especially the sexual. If you're going to transcend anything, transcend your ideas about "spirituality" and embody your humanity. To fully embody your humanity is to feel your connection to humanity everywhere. That, to me, is the essence of spirituality.

You have to learn how to walk in the world with balance. The next three chapters will address specific worldly issues and challenges in the areas of relationships, work, and money. But to find that balance, you must be grounded in your own inner truth.

During those moments when you can take a break from "doing" and being busy, make time to get quiet and still and connect with the spiritual presence that is your true nature. But don't linger too long. Once you've made contact with spirit's healing and renewing power, acknowledge it with a prayer of thanks, then get back to your worldly responsibilities. Remember, the work is to bring God into the world, not abandon the world for God.

A day will come when you'll no longer experience any difference between the spiritual and the material, between transcendent Being and the world of action and human affairs. It will all be one flow, and you'll move, dance, and play in it lightly and confidently.

There will be less "you" as an ego, and more of God, the divine, expressing through you. Your real personality, your unique, authentic self, will shine through, and people will love being around you.

Meditation, the practice of being still and attuning to spiritual presence, leads you to the experience of your authentic self. Self-inquiry, the art of delving into who you are beyond all your ideas about who you are, brings you to the core insight. It's the core insight that brings you to the realization of your true self—the *self* that you really are. This is what is meant by the term "self-realization." It is synonymous with enlightenment, clarity, freedom.

Meditation is the primary spiritual *practice;* the explanation of what is needed for self-realization, or freedom, is the *teaching.* The practice grounds you, makes you steady like a rock, and prepares you for the teaching. The teaching allows you to go deeper into the practice.

There is no way to open up to your true spiritual nature without some form of meditation, contemplation, or stillness. This means sitting down for a period of time each day, preferably in the morning, and again in the evening, and just *being.* As I said in the previous chapter, the mind doesn't have to be totally silent to connect with the energy, but it must slow down. There must be enough space between the thoughts so that the energy can be sensed, so that its presence can be felt.

The energy of spirit is felt as a sense of flow. It is experienced in your body as ease and well-being; in your mind, as clarity and meaning, and in your heart, as love and joy. It is not thinking itself that obstructs the flow—you can still have thoughts floating through your mind—but the persistent sense of "I" or "me," with all its pressing wants, needs, and desires.

Make the desire to be one with spirit your goal, and all your human desires will come into balance and will be taken care of one way or another. It's magical how it works!

## THE BARRIER TO SPIRITUAL AWAKENING

Spirit manifests as light and energy. Light, in the spiritual sense, is consciousness, the illumination that comes to a totally clear mind. Energy is vibration, the movement of atoms and molecules that appears as the forms you see and feel, the sounds you hear, the smells you notice, the qualities you taste.

Light is clarity in seeing, energy is sensitivity in feeling. When *consciousness* (which the yogis call Shiva, the male element) and *energy* (which is Shakti, the female) dance together, the world is created. Or, to say it another way, when Shiva and Shakti make love, reality is born. The world you see, touch, taste, and feel is the result of the union of light and vibration.

The dance goes wrong and everybody suffers when the ego—the "me," with all its demands, judgments, expectations, its need to be "right"—gets in the way. It's the ego that blocks the light and brings darkness. The more contracted the ego—the farther it is from God, the Source—the more suffering the individual experiences.

The ego is like a psychic black hole. It sucks everything, including all light, into it, and nothing can escape. Being around someone with a rigid, controlling ego—especially if you are not yet free of the attachment to your own ego—is dangerous not just to your emotional and spiritual well-being but to your very survival.

The darkness in the world—oppression, tyranny, poverty, violence, suffering—is the result of people having strayed from the light. The difference between dictators and despots and normal people is that the former have strayed so far from the light that they have become completely disconnected from spirit, and thus from the rest of humanity.

To awaken spiritually is to come back to the light. You can't make anyone else do this, however. You can't force another person to become spiritually conscious. To use the dance analogy, you have to begin by first getting yourself in step with the music, the underlying rhythm and harmony. Then it will be easier for others to follow you. By being a light for others, you'll show them the way.

To get in step, to get in the flow, get your self out of the way. This means taking a long, close look at this person you take yourself to be. Start paying attention to the concepts, beliefs, and memories that make up your internal psychological reality—the story of your life.

Notice how you tend to view and judge reality through the filters of your beliefs, biases, and prejudices. It's these filters that prevent you from seeing things anew—from getting a truly fresh perspective.

Your judgments and opinions reinforce your ego, the belief that you are a self, a psychological and emotional entity separate and apart from all the other selves out there. By all means, honor individual wave-ness, both your own and others, but don't forget the ocean, the spiritual energy that is the source of everything.

This next tool came out of an insight I had while hiking one afternoon. I felt good and was in a very expanded, meditative state of consciousness, one that allowed me to see the arising of thought within me—especially the "I," or root thought—with unusual clarity.

This process of witnessing the birth of your own "I" thought is an important prelude to the core insight, because it is the sense of "I," "me," and "mine" that is the main barrier to spiritual awakening.

## TOOL #9

## WITNESSING THE BIRTH OF THE "I" THOUGHT

This can be done sitting, standing, or walking. The main thing is to make it a meditation, an act of conscious contemplation. Begin with the Expanding Awareness technique, so that you get the sense of being the space, the awareness, in which your body lives, in which breathing rises and falls, in which sensations and feelings come and go. Give yourself a little time to get as clear as possible, so that your mind is relatively quiet. Feel yourself to be this expanded awareness, expressing itself through this unique body/mind that is "you."

Then, with your awareness pulled slightly behind and above your head, simply begin to observe the thoughts that come to you. Pay particular attention to where they come from—the space out of which thoughts arise. You'll notice, if you look closely enough and trace an individual thought back to its source, that they come out of nowhere. They are, literally, born out of emptiness, out of nothing. What a marvelous realization!

You can get really specific with this. Don't trace just any thought back to its source, but focus on the "I" thought itself. For example, if a thought like "This is a ridiculous exercise" arises, reframe the thought into the notion it is really expressing, which is "I think this is a ridiculous exercise." Say it a few times to yourself. Then get quiet and still, and let the complete thought "I think . . ." slowly form itself in your consciousness.

As you do this, come back to the sense of yourself as being the awareness, or consciousness, behind the thought. Notice how the thought "I" is just like any other thought. It is born out of nowhere— the vast emptiness of consciousness. Then it seems to take on a so- lidity, a realness to it, as the energy behind it formulates and coalesces into more images and words, into judgments and speculations.

Then, once the thought has expressed itself, if you let it go, it dissolves back into nowhere, to be quickly replaced by another thought. But as you begin to master the art of staying very aware and present like this, the number of thoughts arising in your mind will be fewer, and there will be more space between them. You'll start to experience a more consistent feeling of inner clarity and freedom. Thoughts will come and go, but they won't be a problem.

---

It can actually be an exciting process, tracing the birth of the "I" thought. It's like being a physicist, seeking the origins of the universe, of creation. Except you are doing this in your very own consciousness! You are discovering how "you"—this "I," this "me" that you take yourself to be—are born. And, in discovering the source of your own birth, as a psychological/emotional entity, you are coming to real spiritual freedom.

Indeed, you are coming to something more. You are drawing closer to the most powerful and liberating insight you will ever arrive at in your existence here as a human being: you are coming to understand that this whole universe, as well as all the events and circumstances in *your* experience, are *your* creation.

The universe is your creation in the sense that no matter what happens, you are the one who perceives, who experiences, the reality that is your life. And the clearer your perception, the more right, natural, and harmonious everything will appear to you. It is only when you feel separate and disconnected from your experience that things feel jarring, out of balance, or oppressive in a way that makes you feel like a victim.

Come back, then, to yourself as source. Come back to the awareness of how you, *as* awareness, create your "I" thought, and all the thoughts that follow, including the entire "story" of your life. Realize *that,* and everything in your life will begin to make a whole lot more sense to you.

Then you'll know what the Buddha meant when he said, "All the ten thousand things are created by a single thought." Then you'll be a Buddha yourself. You'll be an awakened human being.

### TEACHERS

On the path to awakening, there will be times when you'll be stuck, and you'll need help. Simply put that thought out to the universe, and then wait. Before long, a teacher—in the form of a person, a book, an event—will appear.

A good teacher has only one mission: to cut as wide a swathe as possible through the field of unconsciousness. He or she can stop your mind, interrupt your habitual patterns of thinking, and open you up to an entirely new perspective or experience. Such a teacher provokes you into taking a long, hard look at yourself, at just who you think you are.

Jean Klein was that teacher for me. When I met him I'd been on my spiritual journey for about ten years, and I had developed the ability, through meditation, to quiet my mind and be more present with my awareness. But I wasn't yet free. I was still seeking. I wanted to be free of self-doubt. I wanted to be in that state of freedom, of expansion, ease, and clarity, all the time. (That was something I learned later from Jean: let go of the attachment to being clear and at ease, and you'll naturally be more clear and at ease!)

When I heard him speak for the first time, there were about sixty of us crowded into the basement of the home where he was staying. I was in the second row. Jean came out looking very elegant in a silk shirt and a cravat, with his white hair swept back along the sides of his head like wings. He was tall, thin, in his seventies. He sat down on a chair placed between two tall vases of very beautiful flowers. An exotic incense was burning.

We spent some time in silence, then he said a few words in his thick European accent. I was eager to ask a question and put up my hand. He turned to me.

"Jean, can you tell us something about your enlightenment, about what actually happened?"

He contemplated my question for what seemed a long time, which I later discovered was not unusual. He wanted you to get a feel for the silence out of which words, questions, and answers came—and back into which they inevitably disappeared. Silence, the subtle yet exquisite vibration of *being,* as he often said, was our true nature.

Then he spoke, slowly and very seriously. "What is the motive for your question?"

I was taken aback. What was the motive for my question? Nobody had ever asked me that before! I mumbled something about the fact that some of us might find it inspiring, or useful, to know what he had gone through.

Then his voice softened. He began to talk about the importance of seeing where questions came from, and getting insight into the "person"—the ego, the psychological/emotional entity who was always seeking support for and reinforcement of its own myth, its story. Thus I was introduced to the enlightenment conversation and the power of self-inquiry—or what I call working with the core insight—to bring about authentic inner freedom.

"Find out who you are beyond all your ideas about who you are," he said, "and you'll discover a happiness, a joy in being, that does not depend upon words, other people, or circumstances. Then that happiness will always be with you, no matter what happens."

In any encounter, the teacher is the one who is most present, yet teachers are not "better" or "higher" than you. They just have been places you haven't gone yet. They are like guides on a river rafting trip. They have been down the river many times before. They know where the rapids are, the dangers and pitfalls. They've also been tossed out of the raft. They know what to do to save themselves from drowning. They have the knowledge and skills—and an unquenchable faith that life will take care of them!

Some spiritual teachers are gifted with psychic abilities, or what the yogis call *siddhis*, magical powers. They may be able to read your energy field, heal illness, see into the future, transmit thoughts or images directly into your consciousness, or evoke dramatic sensory experiences of light, color, or sound.

Such gifts are to be appreciated, but it's important to realize that they actually have nothing to do with enlightenment. Enlightenment is to be free of the attachment to ego. It brings with it a genuine openness, kindness, and humility. If a truly enlightened individual has any of these powers, he or she will use them wisely, and always from a place of unconditional love. You won't feel any sense of being a pawn in someone else's power game.

Stay with the teacher who empowers you, who brings you to your own truth. Avoid the teacher who seeks to disempower and control you, who insists he or she has the answers for you.

There is only one way to tell for sure whether someone is enlightened or not: you have to be fully awake yourself. Then it's easy to detect the contractions in someone's psyche. You see clearly where people are at, the degree to which they are or are not free. You feel it, and there's no judgment about it, just an awareness of what is.

Until you get that clear yourself, keep your feet on the

ground, your heart open, and trust your gut. Be careful, too, of any tendency you may have to project either personal dislike or starstruck reverence out onto others. Both are a barrier to clear seeing.

Real teachers see no difference between you and themselves. They don't actually take themselves to be a "teacher." They don't "take" themselves to be anything. That's why they are so free. They have seen through the illusion of concepts and ideas about self. For them the relationship of student-teacher is only a device, a vehicle for the transmission of the teaching. Their only goal is to help others get free so that suffering can come to an end.

All authentic teachings lead to the realization that you and the teacher are of the one divine energy. When you realize that you are the same beautiful person you took your teacher to be, you'll have understood the teaching. Then the student-teacher relationship dissolves, and you become friends.

The master knows that he or she is always a student, whereas the student still hopes some day to be a master. You'll always remember and honor your teacher as the person who led you back to your Self, the master within, but the distinction won't get in the way of your new relationship.

You'll become a teacher for others, although you won't be attached to the label "teacher." The more you remember how it was to struggle and suffer in your own search for truth, the easier it will be for you to relate to the struggles of others. It will make you a better teacher.

Whenever the situation is asking you to be there as a guide for others, there is only one thing you need remember: just be in the space of oneness, of presence, and the wisdom of the moment will guide you in what to say or do. It never fails.

Seek out friends who share your interest in truth, and then you can support each other. Your friends become your spiritual community. Such friendships endure forever. At the same time, don't spend too long in the company of those who resist change, who are still caught in their egos, in the net of limiting beliefs and concepts. You'll only keep yourself stuck.

The proof that you've understood the teaching is that you'll find your own language for it. As long as you keep repeating someone else's words, or clinging to a set of beliefs or doctrines you learned from an authority outside yourself, you haven't yet got it. Don't give up, though! You'll get it.

No matter how long it seems to take, you will, eventually, wake up to who you really are. You will one day realize that the happiness you've so long sought is in fact your true and constantly abiding nature. And, when you do, you'll shake your head in amazement at the fact that it took so many years to discover something that has been yours all along!

So don't postpone it. Stop reading for a moment, breathe deeply, let your awareness expand. Feel yourself in your body. Feel your own energy. Feel the energy around you. Feel yourself one with the vast ocean of energy and consciousness that is your true nature.

Yes, that's it.

Breathe into it.

Be it.

Be the beautiful person you are.

### TRUST

Erich Fromm, the well-known psychoanalyst, described his friend the Zen master D. T. Suzuki (no relation to Suzuki Roshi) this way: "He was just himself, his thinking rooted in his being." Ah, what a perfectly sensible way to be!

Most people's thinking stems from inside their heads, an automatic mental reaction that ferments up out of the jumble of ideas, opinions, judgments, and beliefs already spinning around in the cranial vault.

But to think from the depths of your being is to think from clarity, stillness, the immense creative spaciousness that is your true self, your spiritual essence. It is to be relaxed and grounded in your body, with your heart open and your mind quiet. Then thinking has a freshness, an originality, an immediacy to it. It is no longer merely intellectual "mind-stuff," but it has a potency and a relevancy to it. It is spontaneous, appropriate, and it *means* something. Not a thought is wasted.

The more you tap the source of your own spiritual depths, the more you trust the innate wisdom of the moment. Spirit, the life force, will guide you every step of the way, once you learn to trust it.

Trust is the hardest lesson for people to get. The material world, with all its distractions and temptations, its threats and its dangers, exerts such a hold on most people that they just don't trust spirit. Compared with the in-your-face reality of the daily struggle to just survive and get ahead, spirit seems somehow just too intangible.

But once you awaken to spirit, you realize it's the most "real" thing there is. Events and circumstances are constantly changing, but whenever you get quiet and still and pause to notice it, spirit is always here. You just need to be open to it. What a blessing it is to know this!

To be open is to be vulnerable. As Krishnamurti used to say, when you are truly vulnerable, you can't be hurt. You can't be hurt because you're not holding on to any image of yourself. You're not attached to any self-concept that can be attacked or invalidated.

Imagine how freeing this is! You don't go around thinking of yourself as being someone special, or someone unworthy, or someone *anything*. You don't hold on to any pictures of yourself at all, so therefore you don't have to worry about defending or justifying yourself.

This goes way beyond self-esteem. Self-esteem is a psychological process that applies to people who still take themselves to be a "somebody," who are trying to feel better about themselves. And if you're going to continue to believe in yourself as a separate psychological entity, it certainly makes more sense to feel better about yourself than to feel worse.

But with true spiritual awakening, there is the gradual dropping away of all concern and obsession with "self," and this allows for the liberation of your true Self. It allows for a sense of yourself that does not depend on beliefs or concepts. It is the sense "Wow, I am just this *being,* this powerful current of awareness, of consciousness, manifesting in this unique body/mind/personality that is *me!*"

Imagine how much freedom such a realization gives you to move in the world, to explore, risk, create, and play. You have complete trust that all your needs will be provided for, and that all problems will work themselves out. This is true abundance, this inner fullness. You care deeply about other people, but you truly do *not* care what they think or say about you. No one any longer has the power to control your thinking, or upset you in any way whatsoever.

Other people's insults, judgments, and negativity may cause a brief ripple in your consciousness—as awake and enlightened as you may be, you still *have* an ego, you still *are* a person—but they pass through, and you quickly come back to the ease and fullness of your inner being.

You come to this kind of consciousness through spiritual awakening, through true self-knowledge. And there's nothing like the mirror of relationships, work, and money to show you just how well you know yourself, and how successfully you're able to integrate your spirituality into everyday life.

Let's look into these wordly mirrors, then.

### CHAPTER FOUR

# Creating Harmony in Your Relationships

## ACCEPTANCE

Creating balance and harmony in your relationships begins within. Your relationships with others are a reflection of your relationship with yourself.

If you don't like yourself much, you'll always be at odds with others. If you accept yourself for who you are, you'll be more accepting of others. When you accept someone for who they are, you have the chance for a really good relationship. If there are things about them you can't accept, you may still be able to have a good relationship—you just may not be able to live together.

Acceptance is the key to successful relationships, so don't get too involved with someone you have difficulty accepting. You're only asking for trouble. Similarly, avoid relationships where you always have to hold yourself in check. If you can't be wholly and completely yourself with the other person, why would you want to be with them?

There are few things in life as satisfying as a good relationship—and few as painful as a bad one. It's a major mistake to get into a relationship thinking or believing someone is going to change. People don't change, fundamentally. They mature, grow wiser, less neurotic—if they work at it. But their basic personality quirks and characteristics remain the same.

Everybody has emotional baggage from the past. In any new relationship, you have to ask yourself, Do I have a sense of what baggage this person is carrying? Am I willing to accept it, to deal with it? The clearer you are about your own baggage, the easier it will be to answer these questions.

John Amodeo, a psychotherapist friend and the author of an excellent book on relationships called *Love and Betrayal,* told me once that it generally takes one to two years for a person's real baggage—their shadow—to emerge. In the meantime, they are just showing you the best side of who they are—as you are with them!

This is why it's generally important not to rush into marriage or some other such commitment. You want to be really clear about who this person is first, and that takes time. Now, if you are clear about who *you* are, and if you have done your own shadow work (that is, you've faced and come to terms with your own inner demons, your fears and insecurities), the process of discovering the other person's shadow can often be shortened to a few months. Sometimes you can see on the very first date what they are struggling with.

The first relationship tool is a powerful way to get at the root of much relationship conflict, and to bring more balance and harmony to the communication you have with the person to whom you're relating. It is based on the notion that what we tend to dislike in other people is usually something we don't like (but are often unaware of) in ourselves.

Psychologists call this "projection," and I'll explore it a little more later on in the chapter. The "mirror" exercise will make it easier to understand this phenomenon, and how you can uti-

lize your understanding to transform the quality of your relationships.

Play with this exercise and you may jump to a whole new
level of insight around yourself and what needs to be done to
see yourself more clearly in your relationships. You'll see, also,
how it relates to the Balancing Perceptions process I shared
with you earlier. The mirror exercise is another way of helping
correct lopsided perceptions so that you can see what is really
going on.

## TOOL #10

### THE RELATIONSHIP MIRROR

Pick something that really bothers you about another person with
whom you have a relationship. It may be your lover, a parent, a
friend, or somebody at work. Then take the issue and turn it around.
If the person is really disorganized and it bugs you to the extent that
you really get upset about it, ask yourself, really honestly. "So how
am I disorganized?"

At first you will probably protest that you are not disorganized,
and that may well seem to be true. But if you probe more deeply
into your own psyche and look at how you run your life, you will
probably discover that, at some level, you're actually very afraid of
being disorganized—and that you have to constantly struggle to
keep it all together. This other person is just reflecting back to you,
in a very obvious way, your own fears about being disorganized and
hopelessly out of control.

Seeing this, understanding it, allows you to stop focusing on
what's "wrong" with the other person—which just pushes them
away and makes them not like you—and frees up your energy to
tend to your own garden, so to speak. As you face your own fears

about your life disintegrating into total chaos, you put yourself on the path to finding real peace and balance within.

You can do this with all the traits that cause distress in you when you see them in others. If it's Mary's impatience, look to see how you are impatient. If it's Bill's rudeness, you can bet that when pushed, you also can be rude. If Dick's stuck-up, aloof manner bothers you, take a long, hard look at your own haughtiness. If you find yourself scornful of someone's struggle with their addictions, look beneath the surface veneer of your control and notice how much struggle is going on inside you around your own addictive tendencies.

---

If you remember this truth—that other people are always reflecting back to you who you are—then you have a beautiful way of getting to know yourself at a very deep and authentic level.

Remember, too, that it is not just the negative that people mirror back to you. They also mirror your positive qualities. At a conscious level, that's why you are attracted to certain people. If you are into working out and keeping your body in top shape, you'll be attracted to people who have the same commitment to their physical well-being. If you have a natural love for silence, the beauty of nature and being, you'll be drawn to people who also demonstrate that love.

As you get clearer and come to greater self-acceptance, you'll "mirror" that acceptance back to others. When you fully awaken to your own inner beauty, your true spiritual nature, you'll see only beauty in others. You'll look right past the surface personal stuff with which other people struggle (because you know now that the "stuff" isn't real—it's the illusion) and you'll see who they really are.

And they'll *feel* seen. They'll be more accepting of themselves, because they feel so accepted by you. This is the way you heal your relationships.

## KNOWING YOURSELF

Relationships are about energy. The more energy you have for each other, and the more energy you generate together, the more dynamic the relationship. That's what chemistry is all about. In the best relationships you have a harmonious chemistry, a chemistry that runs deep. When the energy is flowing smoothly, the relationship works. It feels dynamic, alive, good. It nourishes you both.

Relationships are like gardens. If you don't water your garden, if you don't nurture your relationship, it dies from neglect. If you trample all over it, if you dump a lot of anger into your relationship, it dies from abuse.

Tend your relationships with care, just as you would your garden. To extend the garden metaphor: like a plant rooted in the proper soil, you grow best when you're in a relationship that supports your being who you are.

People struggle in their relationships so often because they don't really know themselves. Relationships are relatively effortless when you know who you are, when you are inwardly free. A relationship is very much an inside job. You can't open up to intimacy with another until you're intimate with yourself. This means knowing yourself at the very deepest levels.

In a good relationship, you know where you stand with the other person. You can trust him or her. To get to this level of certainty, you have to know where *you* stand. What do you stand for? If you keep attracting people who are not good for you, look at the kind of energy you're putting out.

When relationships are based on trying to fill some need or longing within you, your vision gets distorted. You don't see the other person clearly. You don't get a sense of their shadow side. At some point in the relationship, it'll display itself, and there will be problems. The negative traits you've chosen to overlook or have failed to see will, sooner or later, surface and bite you in the rear—sometimes with a vengeance.

Three powerful forces make people blind: fear, greed, and sexual desire. You must know yourself well in order to see to what extent these primal urges are running you. You're able to see others more clearly when you know and trust yourself— and when you're not coming from desperation, false hope, or idealism.

To think that trusting someone means believing they won't hurt or betray you is a naive understanding of trust. Real trust is seeing someone else clearly, feeling them at a heart level, and then trusting them to be true to their nature.

If someone tends to be unreliable and dishonest, you can trust them to continue to be that way. If they are a straight-shooter, you can trust them to deal fairly with you. When you first meet someone, it may not be clear whether you can trust them or not. Go with your first impression, your gut instinct, and then be open to a different perspective as the relationship unfolds.

It doesn't hurt to give people the benefit of the doubt, at least initially. But if your instincts are telling you the other person isn't being honest, they're probably not. If it looks like a duck, walks like a duck, and quacks like a duck, it probably is a duck.

Remember, the only games you ever want to play in a relationship are the ones you *both* want to play. Just make sure you agree on the rules!

## COMMUNICATION

Relationship has three important elements—connecting (which is the energy attraction), listening, and sharing from your heart. It's a dialogue. To engage in a conversation with someone is to have a relationship.

Good conversation can admit a little gossip now and then. Gossip, like vanity, is a very human trait. It feeds the ego—and there's nothing wrong with tossing the ego a bone once in a while! In the end, though, vanity and gossip are like candy. They don't really satisfy, and too much can make you sick.

Deep and honest communication—sharing the truth— keeps the energy flowing in a relationship. It is the lifeblood of relationship. The problem is that people are so often afraid to tell the truth. Or they don't know how to. Or they don't want to hear it. If you want to grow and become free, you have to listen to what you'd probably rather not hear.

The truth is what you're experiencing. It's what cannot be argued with, as in "I'm hungry," "I'm confused," or "I don't like what's happening." It's what you experience in your body, in the form of sensations, feelings, emotions. Nobody can invalidate these. They're true for you.

If you let people invalidate your own inner experience, it shows you don't yet trust yourself. You don't yet know yourself. If you keep getting criticism or negative feedback from a lot of different people, it's time to sit up and start listening. Your universe is telling you something.

The truth can't be used as a weapon for beating your partner over the head. That's the ego's way, its need to be "right." The truth is what's in your heart. You communicate your heart's truth with sensitivity and love. This is how people befriend each other.

Your "personal" reality, or story, is made up of your beliefs, opinions, judgments, history. This is the particular way you've chosen to see reality. If it's very different from the personal reality of the one you're in relationship with, the two of you are probably going to be at odds with each other. Being on the same wavelength, sharing similar personal realities—with enough differences to spark some interesting energy between you!—makes for a happy and harmonious relationship. This is the essence of compatibility.

When you both feel a connection to the larger reality beyond your personal preferences and beliefs—to the deeper energy of life itself—then you have a spiritually rich relationship. You may honor and share your individual stories, but you won't let them get in the way of what really matters. Then there's no end to the depths you can plumb together.

The deepest communication always comes out of silence. True communication leads back to silence. To be totally present, without any agenda, is the highest form of relationship. You get to this place by first being *honest* about your agenda—your emotional baggage, your issues, concerns, and considerations. You have a truthful, sensitive dialogue about it. The withheld energy is cleared, the relationship feels lighter. Understanding dawns.

When you understand each other, there's nothing more to be said, at least in that moment. You find yourself sharing an energy, a presence, that's beyond words. When you're both at ease with silence, you connect at a level words alone can never take you to. Then the communication becomes telepathic. A look, a gesture, a touch is enough. This is true intimacy.

A friend, Web, has a beautiful definition of love: it is the desire to understand another. It's being interested enough in the other person to *want* to understand them. People want, more than anything else, to be listened to, heard, understood. You give someone a great gift when you listen to them. When you love someone, you listen to them.

Sadly, people so often don't listen. On a personal note, I can say that for much of my early adult life, I didn't listen very well, especially to women. I had no trouble listening to men, especially powerful, successful men. After all, I wanted to be one of them, so I was eager to learn everything I could. I hung on their every word. I suspect many men in our culture have been conditioned like this.

But with women, it was different, and although several partners had pointed out to me over the years that they felt completely unacknowledged and unlistened-to by me, I just didn't get it. Then, one year, I took my girlfriend back to New Zealand, where I was born and raised.

We were staying with my mother, and one afternoon the three of us were standing in the living room of my mother's small flat in Milford, in the midst of a conversation. I remember it as clearly as if it were yesterday.

My mother was talking about something and was going on at some length. I saw my girlfriend look impatiently at me, and her expression spoke loudly—"You're not listening to her!"—and I realized I wasn't. In fact, it dawned on me that I had tuned her out completely—and had done so from the moment she started talking.

What was more shocking to me was that I suspected I'd been tuning her out for most of my life since my teenage years. (I guess I learned it from my father, who was so caught up in his own struggles that he was not emotionally available to my mother.) I inwardly shook myself, breathed down into my belly, made eye contact with my mother, and started listening. She, in turn, got more focused with what she was saying. I heard her, and she felt heard. When she finished saying her piece, she visibly relaxed, and it seemed that we had met each other on a whole new level.

A few years later, I was talking to her on the phone late at night. She was in New Zealand, and I was calling from my home in California. Mum was telling me about some things that were bothering her and making her life pretty miserable. As she talked I noticed, again, that my attention was wandering. I somehow had trouble getting interested in listening to her tale of woe.

Then I heard an inner voice: 'Jim, your mother is really suffering right now. No one else is there for her. Maybe you could open your heart and listen."

Again, I forced myself to be present. I let my heart open to her. "Tell me all about it, Mum," I said, with all the love that I really did feel for her. Immediately, she lightened up, and within a few minutes she was telling me about something else, and laughing like a young girl again. It felt so good to hear her sounding happy!

That phone call shifted our relationship to yet another level, and ever since, there has been a special quality of affection between us. It has felt good and right, too, to relate to my mother not so much as "mother" but as a woman who has her own feelings, needs, desires, hopes, and wishes—as a woman who has her own story to tell.

The lesson from all of this? People *do* lighten up, they do get focused, when you really listen to them. And there's a magic that happens as well. That was something I learned in my practice as a healer many, many years ago. Patients would come in and tell me about their problems and worries, and if I just listened to them, if I opened my heart to them so there was a palpable energy of caring, of love, in the treatment room, sometimes I wouldn't even have to say or do anything. Their eyes would brighten, they'd breathe deeply, smile (perhaps after crying a little first), and say something like, "Gosh, I feel better now."

It's funny, you listen and let people tell their story, and in the very telling, they are already beginning to let it go. They are becoming free of the past. But if you don't listen to them, they keep clinging to their story like a life raft, and they never get free of it (unless they are extraordinarily spiritually self-motivated).

The following tool is the best one that I've come across for consciously deepening the quality of communication in a relationship. It's good to do it with your partner, or even your child, if you can make a game out of it, and thus coax them into participating.

### TOOL #11
### BALANCED COMMUNICATION

Set aside fifteen to twenty minutes for this. Sit facing each other in silence, close your eyes, breathe, relax, and get centered in your own being. Get in touch with whatever thoughts, ideas, or feelings you wish to communicate to your partner. Then open your eyes and be very present with each other in an intentional, but soft-eyed, compassionate way. One person goes first, and for the next five to ten minutes, shares whatever is on their mind. Make only "I" statements when you do this. Speak only of your own experience and what is true for you, as in "I've been feeling a lot of joy (or sadness) lately," or "I notice that I am confused about some issues, and want to talk about them," or "There's something I need to get off my chest."

The idea is not to make the other person wrong in any way. It's not about, as they say in AA, "taking the other person's inventory." You're just sharing what's so for you. If you are the other person, you simply listen, using your breath to help you stay relaxed, focused, and present. Keep your heart and mind open. Not only do you not say anything, try not to mentally analyze or judge what your partner is sharing. Just hear them. This is active listening.

When your partner has finished speaking, thank them for sharing, and they thank you for listening. Then feed back to them the gist of what you heard them saying. Preface your feedback with the words "This is what I heard you saying . . ." (The partner sharing may have had a whole number of things they just needed to say, or there might have been a particular point they wanted to get across.) It's also important to acknowledge any feelings they may have shared, as in. "It sounds like you feel really upset . . ." or "It sounds like you're really excited about/afraid of what might happen . . ."

The partner receiving the feedback just acknowledges the accuracy of it with a yes or no. If it's the latter, he or she can rephrase the essence of the communication to clarify what was being said, until there is understanding, so that the energy between you feels clear and balanced. Then you pause again, take some time out for meditative silence and centering, and then switch roles. The person who spoke first becomes the active listener, and it is the listener's turn to speak.

---

You can employ the basic skills of this exercise whenever you're in communication with anyone, whether you're at work, at lunch, on a bus, or standing in line for coffee. The key elements are being present and focused, listening actively, and checking to make sure you understand clearly what the other person is saying—which presupposes, of course, that you are clear about your own communication.

For example, whenever I'm listening to someone and he or

she is not being absolutely clear (at least to me), I will gently say something like, "I don't quite understand you. Could you say more about that?" or "Could you elaborate?"

It requires only one person to be centered, grounded, and very present in their listening and their speaking, and the other person will, much of the time, spontaneously improve the quality of their own communication. The stronger, clearer energy always influences, in a positive way, the less clear, more scattered energy.

This is also true of group meetings or encounters where the communication may be getting out of hand. One solid, grounded presence can shift the energy of the whole group and bring it into greater harmony and balance.

You can do an enormous amount to transform the quality of *all* your relationships by getting very clear about these ground rules of communication.

### CHILDREN

Children, too, need to be listened to, to be heard. Children who are encouraged from the beginning to trust their feelings, to listen to their inner code, and to be aware of the deeper spiritual energy underlying existence, grow up feeling secure within themselves. They are able to evolve the story of their young, growing life in a healthy way (a necessary part of ego development), but because they are so connected to life at a feeling level, they don't get lost in their story. They are less likely to mistake the story for reality. Imagine how much easier your journey would be if you'd been given that gift!

John Bradshaw, therapist and teacher, said that children need three things from their parents—time, energy, direction. Every conscious parent knows this is true. If you have children, you may sometimes find yourself begrudging the time and energy they need. This is normal and human. Yet when you look back at what you've given your children, you never regret it. And your kids will always remember and be grateful.

A parent's greatest happiness is to see his or her children happy. As a parent, I know from experience that the best thing I can do to ensure my son's happiness is to be there for him in body, mind, and spirit. The best thing I can do is to love him. I learned a long time ago that if Adam was suffering, for whatever reason—not doing well at school, feeling rejected by his peers, or just feeling withdrawn—there was one solution that always worked (and still does, to this day): I simply remind myself to "pour as much love into him as possible."

The single most important secret to being a good father, I feel, is to keep opening my heart to my son. At the same time, I give him a lot of space to be himself. I give him a long leash so that he has room to explore his world—and, every once in a while, if he looks like he's getting into trouble, I gently but firmly rein him back in. Through being given the freedom to grow and find himself in this way, I believe, he will best come to wholeness and balance in his own being. It has been true so far.

When Adam's mother and I were going through our divorce (he was six at the time), one of the factors motivating me was that I didn't want him seeing us continually fighting. I'd grown up with that. I'd lived in a household filled with tension for much of my childhood, and it had had a major disturbing effect—as you might imagine—on my psyche. No wonder I was so obsessed with finding inner peace in later life.

If you're considering divorce and you have children, it's always a difficult decision. Their happiness matters tremendously, but they're not going to be happy unless you are, too. The long-term happiness of everyone involved has to be considered.

The negative fallout of divorce is minimized when both parents can put aside their personal differences and make a genuine, loving effort to be there for their children. Adam's mom and I have done that for him. It makes me respect and appreciate her in a way that I wasn't able to when I was married to her—another example of how good can come out of an event that might previously have been thought of as a disaster, or a failure.

Children pick up on energy. If you're off-center, out of sync with yourself and your life, it's going to affect your children. It will throw them off-balance. If your children are acting out, check first to see how clear and grounded you are. You owe it to your children to be as centered and as grounded as you can be. Where else are they going to learn this most important living skill, unless you model it for them?

Just how sensitive children are to energy is illustrated in a story that Ed, a friend, told me about his three-year-old daughter, Jacqueline. Jacqueline was sitting at the kitchen table and asked him what a halo was. Ed pointed to a picture of an angel that was hanging up on the kitchen wall. "It's what is called an aura," he said. "When people are in a good place, when they feel loved and nurtured, they get this golden light around them."

Jacqueline considered her father's statement for a moment, and then said, "Yes, and when people get angry, it turns red."

Ed told me that her remark blew him away, because neither he nor his wife, Millie, had talked about auras with Jacqueline before. He laughed sheepishly. "Millie and I were going through a difficult spell recently and things were getting pretty heated. No wonder Jacqueline was frowning. She was seeing all that red!"

Children, we agreed, are tuned in to levels of energy and magic in life with which most adults have long since lost touch.

This work of the heart, of spiritual awakening, is about re-claiming the magic.

## FRIENDSHIP

Relationships, whether with children or adults, are an exercise in courage, honesty, mutual respect, and love. They will always be your greatest teacher—the true measure of your enlightenment.

Genuine communication in a relationship takes vulnerability and trust, a willingness to talk about your needs, desires, feelings, fears. Communication breeds understanding. If what you understand about life doesn't work to bring greater harmony and love into your relationships, it's not worth much. On the other hand, if you don't "understand" much about life and the meaning of it all but you love well and care deeply about other human beings, then you understand the only thing that really matters!

Nobody's perfect. To have problems in your relationships is normal. Face your problems, deal with them, and you'll learn and grow from them. Your relationships will flow more effortlessly, be more satisfying, and you'll develop deep and beautiful friendships.

The Irish poet W. B. Yeats wrote: "Thinkest thou where man's glory begins and ends. My glory was, I had such friends." He knew what mattered in life. In the best relationships, you're each other's friend. You stand by each other. You're there for each other. Imagine a world where the majority of humanity made their personal beliefs secondary and focused instead on being friends—or at least good neighbors—with each other!

If a husband and wife are not each other's best friend, there's not much hope for the marriage. Honesty in your marriage—or in any relationship—is the essential ingredient for friendship. If you're not honest, you're not a true friend.

If the vision of a world where most of us are on friendly terms with each other strikes a chord in your heart, you can start to manifest that vision in reality by learning to be a friend to yourself. Then practice being a friend to those close to you. Then venture out and expand the circle of friendship.

Being a friend to yourself means trusting and accepting your feelings, not judging yourself. It means owning, integrating, all your energies, emotions, impulses. You have to accept yourself as you are before you can make any meaningful changes in your behavior. Otherwise you're always fighting yourself.

You don't have to "love" everyone, or even especially like them. Let's be realistic here. But *do* respect other people's right to exist, to be different, to live their lives the way they see fit. If we all gave that basic respect to each other, we'd have a more peaceful and harmonious world.

Men and women need to learn to be friends with each other. Too often we objectify the opposite sex and fail to see the real person. Too many men still see women primarily as sex objects. Too many women still see men as meal tickets. It's a dynamic that, thankfully, is changing as men and women become more conscious and open up to their true, divine nature.

Men need to learn that they can be both strong *and* soft and nurturing. Women need to learn that they can take charge and be strong without losing their softness. Most men actually know how to be soft and nurturing, but because of their fear and their need to control, they lose touch with their softness. They can get so clear, so detached, that they forget the heart. They cover their softness in a suit of armor—intellectual, emotional, physical. It's their armor that hides their pain. Women's pain, much of the time, is that they see men's armor.

Men and women need to show themselves to each other. They need to respect each other. At some point, they need to get beyond the roles of "man" and "woman," and relate to each other as the spiritual beings they are. Men need to discover the goddess, the feminine element, within them. Women need to discover the god, the masculine element, in them. It's a question of inner balance.

Too many men and women have a certain emptiness inside, the legacy of an incomplete relationship with their fathers and mothers. They run around believing they "need" a partner to fill that void. When you come from need, your relationships are based on emotional dependency, control, addiction. There's an undercurrent of desperation and fear. No wonder so many relationships don't work.

You've got to find the beloved, the friend, within you. This is the real work of healing your relationships—it's creating the inner marriage of masculine and feminine, so that you find wholeness within. It's very much a spiritual journey you're on. Sooner or later, you're going to have to accept that, if you haven't already done so. We're all moving closer to God, to discovering our oneness with the source—and therefore with each other.

As a friend, Liz, said to me once: "Make love to the goddess within, then go find yourself a real person." When, as a result of your spiritual work, that emptiness is finally filled from within so that you no longer need a man or woman to complete you, you'll be able to enjoy being alone. You may still want a partner in your life, but it will no longer be such an urgent need.

The way to accelerate the movement back to inner wholeness is to see through your own story. Master the core insight, get free of the need to be seen or thought of as "somebody" who is special or unique, and all your relationships will be relatively effortless. In fact, the more open, present, and authentic you are, the more likely it is that your lover will treat you as *very* special and unique.

### THE WHOLE ENCHILADA

When you like a lot about a person, but there are things you don't like, try focusing on the positive and not the negative. It'll do wonders for the relationship.

A relationship is the whole enchilada (I learned this piece of wisdom from Adam's mother—a difficult lesson to "swallow," but a much-needed one). You can't just eat the sour cream on top, in other words. However, if the salsa keeps giving you indigestion—that is, if there's something about the other person you just can't abide, and nothing's likely to change because you are just too fundamentally different—you'll probably be happier dining elsewhere.

You can have what you want, you know. Get clear about your tastes. Put your intention out there. Wait. Be patient. You'll be surprised at how the universe will provide. It only takes a divorce or two to realize that it's unwise to settle for less than what you really want. Better to be alone than in an unhappy relationship. In fact, in an unhappy relationship, you usually feel more alone than if you were living by yourself.

Some people just don't do so well together. Relationships are about energy, remember, and some energies don't resonate all that well. Sometimes you're just not meant to live with or love a particular person. You can still respect and like them, though. Probably more so, if you don't have to live with them.

When in doubt as to whether to continue with a certain relationship, ask yourself, Am I really accepted in this relationship? Is it healthy for me? Is this the person with whom I want to spend my life, with whom I can share a vision and create a future? Invite the other person to ask the same questions of themselves.

The signs of trouble in a relationship—as in any area of life—are always evident from the beginning, if you'd but pay attention to them. As one teacher said, If you can hear the whispers, you don't have to listen to the screams. Too many people wait till the house is almost burned down before they jump up to call 911. They lurch from crisis to crisis. It's an emotionally exhausting way to live.

The truth is, you always know whether a relationship is right or not. Deep down, in your heart, your gut, your intuitive core, you can sense it. If the feeling persists over time, you can trust it. It's okay to honor your own feelings, even when it means saying no to someone else. Sometimes, when you're true to yourself, others don't like it and their feelings get hurt. Just remember what Napoleon said on the eve of a battle that was likely to result in heavy casualties: "You can't make an omelette without breaking eggs."

You don't have to explain yourself. Sometimes you can't. It's okay to say, "I don't know why, it's just a feeling I have, and I've learned to trust my feelings." This is a good philosophy to practice whenever you need to say no to anyone.

After all, which pain would you rather deal with—the pain of someone telling you the truth about their feelings, or the pain that comes with realizing you've been lied to and betrayed? If you've ever experienced betrayal, you know the wound takes a long time to heal. Having someone tell you a hard truth hurts, too, but you get over it more quickly.

Be open to hearing the truth, be open to telling it. As my friend Larry puts it: "Full disclosure, made gently, is the way to avert most of the pain and suffering that happens in relationships."

The truth, spoken with a lot of heart, is the key to bringing balance to any relationship.

## FREEING YOURSELF FROM CO-DEPENDENCE

Make sure that you don't give other people the power to control *your* feelings. To do so is to be co-dependent.

Co-dependence is defining yourself by your relationships, by what others think of you. It's censoring your own feelings and behavior so as to not risk hurting someone else's feelings. It's wanting others to like you.

Notice how it's the person who doesn't need approval from others who always gets lots of it. But the person who hungers for approval and is always doing things to try and get it seldom gets any. Such behavior tends to push others away. Nobody likes being around emotionally needy people.

It's like respect. People often complain that they don't feel respected by others, yet the fact is, people respect us when we respect ourselves. Self-respect comes from knowing who you are, what you will and will not stand for, and honoring the feelings and boundaries that matter to you. And *you* are the one who gets to decide what matters in your life.

If your reference for who you are is still outside yourself, it means you're co-dependent. If you dare not do or say something because someone might get angry or sad, you're co-dependent. Staying together because it's "safe," even though neither of you is growing, even though you're not really happy, is co-dependence. In such relationships, the passion, the creative energy, usually dies first. Eventually you may even stop caring about each other.

Co-dependence is unhealthy. It poisons relationships. To be co-dependent is to be a "phony." It's to be less than authentic. If it's still in your makeup, get into therapy or do whatever it takes to get free of it. You owe it to yourself.

Co-dependence is the result of the hurts and wounds of childhood. Before a man can really be with a woman, he must heal his wound around his mother, otherwise he keeps putting his mother's face on every woman he meets. Similarly, a woman must heal her relationship with her father, so that she doesn't keep seeing "Dad" in every man she meets.

The mother/father wound is the place in us that nobody else can fill. It is the result of a primal longing for the ideal parents, the parents who would always be there for us, who could do no wrong, and who would take care of us forever. When you understand the nature of this wound and recognize it in yourself, you see why people project so much onto others. You see why they idealize their lover, their therapist, their teacher, their minister.

The wound is healed through facing yourself, through facing your own inner pain, your emptiness, your disappointment, your need for love, affection, security. You can do this in therapy. You can do it sitting in meditation, by breathing into and allowing the negative feelings and images to come into your awareness, and then releasing them.

The most effective way to heal the emotional legacy of childhood is to observe yourself in your relationships. Notice what causes you to attack or withhold. Notice the words you use. Notice the feelings and sensations that come up in your body as you get close to another person. Notice your fears around intimacy.

Notice the way in which you judge or form conclusions about the other person, the decisions you make about who they are in order to get them neatly pegged in your own mind. Start pulling those projections back in, back home, where they belong. This is an essential ingredient in relationship healing.

What you say about the other person usually says more about you than it does about them. The fact is you can't change the other person, and it's a total waste of energy to try—not to mention the fact that it drives an even deeper wedge between you. (How do *you* feel when someone tries to tell you how you should be?)

How others choose to live and behave is their decision and responsibility. But you *can* change yourself. To change yourself, stop focusing on what's wrong with the other person and start taking a long and deep look at yourself.

When you finally face the fact that you—not your mother, your husband, your boyfriend, or any other person—are the problem in your life, then you're on your way to freedom.

Heal yourself through finding your own inner freedom, and then bring that consciousness into your relationships. The whole dance will change, and you'll get an entirely new sense of what's possible. If the other people in your life choose not to look at themselves, it won't bother you. That's their right. You'll learn to accept them for who they are. You'll have compassion for their suffering, but you won't get hooked into it. You'll spend time with them—or you won't.

You can't save anyone. Even though it may hurt to see another person suffering emotionally, you can't take their suffering away. You may be able to give someone an emotional Band-Aid, but in the end they're going to have to face and work through their own suffering. The most you can do is be there as a friend.

Let your reference for who you are come from within you. How else are you going to be true to yourself?

## THE HEALING POWER OF FORGIVENESS

Forgiveness is the key to healing relationships, but there's a difference between trying to forgive and actually forgiving. Usually when people try to forgive, it's premature. They start affirming "I forgive so-and-so . . ." while underneath their good intentions there's still a lot of emotional conflict.

If this is the case with you, you need to feel your pain and anger first. Underneath anger is hurt. The acknowledgment that you've been hurt paves the way for acceptance of whatever it is that happened. With acceptance, there's the chance for real forgiveness.

To come to forgiveness, you usually need to create some space between yourself and the other person. It's hard to lick your wounds when you're still in direct contact with the other person. As you allow yourself to breathe through and feel your pain, the hurt feelings subside. You must also begin to let go of the emotionally charged memories, thoughts, and pictures. This helps bring more clarity. You come back to yourself. Then it is easier to be with the person who hurt or wronged you.

Forgiveness happens naturally once the wounds have begun to heal and you've made a conscious effort to let go of the painful memories that keep the past alive. There's a very good technique, a loving-kindness meditation, that can be helpful here:

### TOOL #12
### FORGIVENESS

When you're in the middle of feeling your pain and hurt, there's nothing to do but breathe into and feel it, until it begins to ease up somewhat. During those times when you're experiencing a little freedom from the pain, sit quietly and visualize the other person.

Experiment with opening your heart to them. See if you can look beyond their hurtful behaviors, the mistakes they've made, the ways in which they've misjudged you, or failed to see who you really are. Try and see the basic goodness in them—the goodness from which they themselves may be disconnected. Try and see that they, too, are struggling to be whole. Remember that every person is following the call of their own soul, whether they consciously realize it or not—and that includes this person who hurt you. The truth is, their journey is at least as difficult as yours, and maybe even more so.

Acknowledge the anger you feel, and then, as you hold them in your mind's eye, affirm something like: "I don't like what you did, and it may be a while before I trust you again, but my own happiness and well-being are what's important to me now. I am going to consciously release you from my energy field and focus on finding peace within myself."

An affirmation along these lines will help you let go of attachment to this person. It will help you expand into a more *impersonal* awareness, where you are not taking them or their actions so personally. You'll begin to let go of the story you've built around them, their hurtful actions, and your own pain. In this way you'll move toward freedom.

---

Practice this meditation and a day will come when you can think of the person who caused you so much pain, and that old emotional charge won't be there. You'll be able to look at them with more detachment, more compassion, more understanding of the pain they were in.

If somebody then asks you, "Have you forgiven so-and-so?"

you'll be surprised to realize that, yes, you have. The fact that you no longer blame them or bear them any ill will is the proof of your forgiveness.

Forgiveness is an inner process. The other person doesn't have to be there. When you think of them, just allow yourself to process the feelings, the grief. In quiet moments, consciously release the memories and pictures that have been keeping the pain alive. Let go of the story that has become so much a part of your life.

Letting go of resentment, hurt, and blame is tremendously liberating. It's imperative, if you're to be happy within yourself, and if you're to find happiness in your relationships.

### FALLING IN LOVE

People make the mistake of falling in love blindly. They trip and stumble into it, without really checking the other person out fully first. They give their heart on a platter. When the relationship sours, their heart gets chewed right up, then spit out! The young make this mistake often, and the middle-aged are not immune to it, either.

When you're standing at the edge of the relationship abyss called "love," it's a good idea to handcuff one arm to the guardrail just to make sure you don't fall in. Love addicts may need to handcuff both arms—and chain a leg as well! When you're good and ready and as sure as you can be that this person is right for you, then you can unlock the cuff and let yourself go. Remember, *you* have the key.

Falling in love is a decision, although it's one that most people make unconsciously. They are not yet aware of that hole inside them—the mother/father wound I spoke of earlier—and how, for true spiritual growth it needs to be filled from within. Thus they tend to go from relationship to relationship, desperately seeking what can only ultimately be found within themselves.

Fall in love consciously, and you'll always be okay, even if the relationship doesn't work out. The healthiest way to do this is to open your heart to that someone special and invite them in. Then you can merge with the other, but you still have yourself, and they still have themselves. It's a joining of two whole people, coming together to make a greater whole. If it's true love, you're probably not going to have too much say in it anyway. The energy will just overtake you. So, be overtaken . . . but be *aware* that you're being overtaken!

Someone once asked Jean Klein what would happen if everybody in the world got enlightened. He paused a moment, then answered with a grin, "Why, then there would only be dancing!" That describes perfectly what a happy relationship is: it's a delightful dance of energies. You're in tune with each other.

When you put aside all the pros and cons, the pluses and minuses, and all the rationalizations, there's only one reason to be in a relationship—because you *want* to be. You really dig each other. When you have this kind of strong mutual attraction, respect, and liking, a relationship is relatively easy. You're both totally committed to finding a way to work your problems out, so that the energy you enjoy together can continue to thrive and grow.

The connection breaks down when, as is so often the case, one or both parties have a foot out the door. You, or your partner, are not really sure whether you want to be in the relationship. You owe it to each other to be really clear, to ask of yourself, Do I really want to be here or not? Keep asking, keep confronting what is so for you, until you do get clear.

If you've tried for enough years to make your relationship work, to get in tune with each other, and it's just not happening, you may be better off parting. You'll have a chance for real happiness living apart, and you may yet be friends.

People jump into relationships too quickly, and they quit too quickly. They do it because they don't know themselves. They live reactively, impulsively. Everybody does it at some time or other. The smart ones learn.

## THE ZEN OF SEX

A lot of the pain and imbalance in relationships is a direct result of the failure to understand the true nature of sex. When you have sex with someone, you energetically bond with them, whether you mean to or not. There's a joining and mingling of your energies and, if you are at all sensitive, you pick up on this, you feel it.

For example, if a man is tense and angry and uses sex as a way of unloading, of releasing, a woman who is sensitive is going to feel used. If a woman with a partner has another lover and is more emotionally drawn to him, her regular partner, if he is sensitive, is going to notice that she isn't really present with him.

This energetic perspective helps explain, at least in part, the current prevalence of AIDS and other sexually transmitted diseases. The sexual freedom and promiscuity that had its beginnings in the sixties and peaked in the late seventies and early eighties saw a breaking down of sexual barriers. Seemingly, everybody was having sex with everybody.

There was little or no concern or respect for boundaries, for whose fluids, whose energies, were mingling with whose. When you stop respecting boundaries, boundaries break down—both energetically and at a cellular level. And without the boundaries to stop them, viruses and bacteria can freely pass through.

It is a wise and sexually responsible person who, before en-
gaging in sex with anyone, not only practices safe sex, but also
says, "Now, do I *really* want to share my sexual energy with this
person? Do I really want to allow them into my energy field in
that way?"

The other main area of confusion around sexuality—and
this is a big one—is that people confuse sex and love, when in
fact they are two different things. You don't have to love someone to enjoy sex. It's a perfectly fine exchange of energies when
two conscious people can get together and enjoy sex for its own
sake. As a woman friend said to me once, "Look, I'm in the middle of a divorce, and I'm not interested in a relationship or
falling in love. If we can have a friendship with some hot sex,
that'll be fine by me."

Problems develop when people don't have this kind of clarity. They meet, they get sexual with each other, they start to become bonded, and then suddenly all their repressed needs and
longings come to the fore. They start getting attached—even
obsessed or addicted—and, before they know it, their deep
need for the connection that they don't have with their inner
selves causes them to "fall" in love.

The freedom to really enjoy sex for its own sake is, like the
ability to fall in love consciously, the result of deep inner clarity and self-knowing. Sexual inhibitions stem from unconscious ego patterns, a "me" that's so contracted in certain areas
that it can't let go. The freer you are of your ego, and the freer
your lover is, the more fun you'll have together. If you have
good chemistry, you'll have great sex. Sex is an energy dance, a
wonderful way to share your love with another person. Making
love can be very spiritual, very deep, or it can just be light, a fun
way to play.

Sometimes people on a spiritual path wonder if they need
to be celibate. If you're controlled by your sex drive and it's dif-

ficult for you to relate to a man or woman without sex getting in the way, then a period of celibacy is useful. It gives you time to see exactly what this energy, which has become such a dominating influence in your relationships, is.

You don't have to give up sex to become enlightened. That's a belief held by those who are still caught in the split between the spiritual and material. You just have to give up the *attachment* to it, the addictive need for it. That's the key. Then your sexual energy finds its natural balance, and sex itself becomes just a spontaneous expression of your true nature. As a tantric Zen master might say, Eat when hungry, sleep when tired, make love when horny!

Sexual energy, when not channeled appropriately, can really mess you up. It plays havoc with your internal chemistry. An enlightened sexuality is one that allows all the room in the world for sexual expression, but always spontaneously, naturally, appropriately. If your sexual energy keeps leaking out in negative ways, you've got a problem. It's something you need to look at. Few things are more of a turnoff than leaky sexual energy.

People have innumerable hang-ups around sex—guilt, fear, inhibition, a Pandora's box of social and religious conditioning. As you work to get free of any complexes or obsessions you may have, keep asking yourself, "Who is it that has these problems?" As you get freer of "self" concern, the problems and inhibitions will start to drop away.

Sexual compatibility is a matter of chemistry—and preferences. Some say the best sex is when you're so attuned to each other that it feels like you're making love with yourself. I would say the best is when it feels like you're making love with the divine. Or the divine is making love with you. In the best sex, you're merged in the heart, both riding the same wave of ecstasy.

Sweetness is a precious quality in a relationship. It's pure heart energy. It's the ingredient that turns friendship into intimacy, the sugar that ferments love. No wonder we call that special person our "sweetheart." Lust has its place. It satisfies our animal nature—and the animal needs to be fed once in a while! But making love with your sweetheart has to be the most satisfying sex.

In a conscious relationship, the sexual fire is experienced in the body, but it is fanned by the heart and soul—and by the quality of communication, both verbal and nonverbal, you share. Truth is the ultimate aphrodisiac. If you have to indulge in fantasies to get turned on to your partner, you're missing a vital connection. However, if you like to fantasize once in a while as a way of enhancing the connection you already have, then you're being creative.

When you're young, there's often no such thing as bad sex (for men, at least!), but as you get older, you tend to become more discriminating. Getting your sexual energy into balance is one of the blessings of age. It allows you to go deeper spiritually with your lover.

It also frees up your creative energy from being obsessed with or addicted to sex, which makes it easier for you to come to real inner peace and freedom and get on with other interesting things in your life.

### THE SECRET OF GREAT RELATIONSHIPS

When you've gone through enough relationships, enough divorces, you realize that unless you can have what really matters to you in a relationship, you'd rather be alone. Before you can be in a conscious and truly fulfilling relationship, you must have learned how to be happy being alone—or else you must discover that ability to be alone within the context of your relationship.

You've got to be willing to walk away from a relationship before you can have it. This is true of anything you really want. You've got to be able to say a firm no before you can say a strong yes. The fact is, if more people realized what a beautiful relationship they could have with themselves, they wouldn't remain in unfulfilling relationships.

In the end, relationships are what you and the other person make them. If there's a battle raging between you, or things are unhappy in some way, you'd better sort it out. Or say good-bye. But be sure of one thing—there's no cavalry coming over the hill to save you. If it's not working for you, it's probably not working for the other person, either.

You're responsible for your relationships. You and the one with whom you're in a relationship. It's up to the two of you. Totally. This responsibility becomes less burdensome, however, the more you allow the energy of spirit to guide you in your relating.

When you try to make a relationship happen, it seldom works. The attempt to control or manipulate the outcome of a relationship comes from fear and insecurity. The best way to manage a relationship is to let it unfold. If there's something real between you, you'll know. When you need to step in and take the initiative, you'll know that, too.

The degree to which a relationship thrives is dependent upon your willingness to face and deal with the inevitable stresses and changes, the stages and cycles, that all relationships go through. Communication is the key to balance, to keeping the energy moving in a productive way.

Commitment is about being committed to the *truth,* not to some concept of forever. Realizing this is part of coming into adulthood. Then you no longer need to fear the "C" word. The real commitment is to be present—right here, right now. It's trusting the quality of your connection, and the wisdom of the moment, to guide you. Your future together, whatever it will be, will flow naturally out of that. If you really love each other, you may well plan to spend your life together. But, if you're wise, you'll both know that there are never any guarantees.

If you're wondering whether a particular relationship—or any other venture—is going to work out or not, you can be sure of one thing: it either will—or it won't. If it isn't working, be honest. Tell each other the truth. Have respect for each other. Then you can part, if not as friends, at least not as enemies—and maybe one day you'll become friends.

If it *is* working, be grateful. Give thanks—to each other, and to the mystery, the power, the grace that makes it all possible. Remember not to take each other for granted, and your love and friendship will grow. This is the main secret of finding balance, harmony, and joy in your relationships.

### CHAPTER FIVE

# Finding Your Work

## A SPIRITUAL EXERCISE

At its best, work is a vehicle for expressing your creative energy, for giving form to spirit, your true nature. It is an opportunity to be present to the moment at hand. It is meditation in action.

Work keeps the material universe ticking. Think of the law of entropy, which, in essence, can be summed up as "Things run down." Without work to either maintain what has already been set in motion or create new movement, what is created will eventually fall into disrepair and decay. Work is an essential process for keeping the material world in balance.

Without work, most people wouldn't earn the money they need to survive, let alone prosper. You may not yet be doing the work you love, but learning to be grateful for the work you have is a step in the right direction. It helps, too, if you view your work as a *spiritual* exercise. Appreciate it as an opportunity to find yourself and to serve, as well as to earn money.

"Right livelihood" is a Buddhist term that refers to earning your living through work that causes no harm, that supports the well-being of people and the environment. It is less about finding a particular kind of work, than it is about doing the work you already have with an attitude of love and service. Remember, it's not so much what you do, but the consciousness with which you do it that counts.

During my early years in chiropractic practice I struggled with my work. I really wanted to be a writer, and I often felt trapped and stressed being confined to the small treatment rooms in my office, working with people in pain.

But chiropractic had a lot to teach me, especially about getting out of my head and being grounded in my body, and about listening to others and developing compassion for their suffering. I was well on my spiritual path and I wanted enlightenment, I wanted freedom. The conflict I experienced around my work as a healer just showed me where I wasn't yet free. I'd often say to myself, "Now, if I were a Zen master, how would I handle my practice and relate to my patients?" One thing always became clear: a Zen master wouldn't complain. He would either do the work with real awareness, or mindfulness, or he'd go do something else!

Most people find their main sense of identity through their work. Work builds self-esteem, for both men and women. However, from the perspective of spirituality, to rely on your work for your identity, for your sense of who you are, is a mistake. Such reliance stops you from diving deep into the core of your own being and finding out who you *really* are. Looking solely to your work for your identity and self-esteem actually increases the potential for experiencing imbalance and stress in your life. If your identity depends upon your work, then it's all very well as long as you remain employed, but what if you get laid off?

One of my friends was a successful magazine editor for almost two decades, and then the magazine he worked for folded. He was unable to find work for two years. He told me how embarrassed he felt, going to parties and other social gatherings, and having people ask him, "So, what do you do?"

"I felt like a leper," my friend told me. "As soon as I said I was out of a job, the men especially would mutter a few inconsequential things, and then say something about needing to go off and freshen their drink, or talk to somebody else. That just made me feel even more depressed. I never realized how much of my identity was tied up in being able to say that I had a job."

My friend was eventually able to use his writing and communication skills to find work in the wine industry, where he has been an executive for many years now, but his experience is far from unique. Unemployment, or the threat of it, is never far away for most people in the corporate world these days. And being self-employed is no guarantee of economic security, either, given all the challenges of making it successfully in a business of one's own.

This is a critical point to understand in terms of finding the balance between the material dimensions of your life and your inner, spiritual well-being. As long as your identity, your psychological and emotional security, depends on what you *do*— that is, having a job, position, or title in life—rather than who you *are,* true inner peace and happiness will always elude you. Your identity will be intact and you'll experience a feeling of well-being as long as you have work, but lose your job, and you lose yourself—or, at least, a major part of yourself. Like my friend the former editor, you'll be in danger of being overwhelmed with feelings of alienation, fear, and depression.

The central theme of this book is to guide you to the core insight, to the realization that you are *not* your thoughts, emotions, beliefs, personal history—nor are you your work. It is this understanding that will set you free and allow you to move in the world—in every dimension of your life, including your work—without stress, with genuine ease and balance.

There are always things you can *do* to create more outward balance in your life, but the real key to stress-free living is learning how to *be*—how to be balanced, centered, and grounded within yourself. Master that, and then what to *do* tends to happen naturally and effortlessly.

Here is a tool that will help free you from being so identified with your work. It will facilitate your moving closer to the place where work can become a true expression of who you are—a vital, necessary, and life-sustaining expression—but it will not *be* who you are.

Then, no matter what happens with your work, you will always be okay. Imagine just how good that will feel!

## TOOL #13

## WHO WORKS?

In the first part of this exercise you'll use the Balancing Perceptions process, so you'll need a sheet of lined paper (or your word processor). Begin by taking a few minutes to breathe into your belly and center yourself. Get quiet, tuned-in to the space around the objects you see, the energy behind the sounds you hear. As you breathe, be aware of yourself as the clear, stable awareness that is always present behind the flow of thoughts, feelings, events, and circumstances.

On the left side of the paper, at the top, write something like, "What I don't like about my job/work." If you're unemployed, write "What I don't like about being unemployed." Then proceed to list all the responses you come up with. Probe deeply into your psyche to find out what is really bothering you, what your objections and considerations are. Put them all down. Keep going until you feel like you've got them all, or at least the main ones.

Once more, take some time to breathe, center, detach. Come back to the fullness of your own being. (If it's hard for you to tap into that fullness, don't worry. This exercise will help you edge closer to it.) Then, on the other side of the paper, counter every negative you wrote down with a positive. Ask yourself, "So, how does this serve my growth? What's the hidden blessing, or gift, here?" Look deep to find it. Here are three examples, with the negative first, and then the positive:

1. "I hate my boss. He's so controlling and insensitive." ("This is an opportunity for me not to be so reactive. I can remember to breathe and just let his energy pass through" and/or "He mirrors the ways in which I can be controlling and insensitive with others.")

2. "I can't be myself at work. If I told them what I really felt, I'd get fired." ("I can be myself inwardly, without needing validation from my work or other people. I can learn how to communicate my truth in ways that are nonthreatening to people.")

3. "Never mind identity . . . I don't have a job, my savings are almost depleted, and I'm about to be out on the street." ("I'd rather not be out on the street, so this is teaching me to get really focused and demonstrate my ability to procure some kind of work, any kind, to bring in money. Later, I can give serious thought to the work I'd most love to do.")

Once you've balanced the positives and negatives, pause to breathe and center yourself again. The second part of this exercise is to write down and contemplate the following affirmations (or use your own words to express the same essential ideas):

"My work is an expression of who I am, but it is not *who* I am."

"My inner peace and happiness come from within. They are expressions of my true spiritual nature and do not depend on my work."

"My work is an opportunity to discover and express my true nature even more deeply."

Stick these affirmations up somewhere where you can see them (the fridge, your bathroom mirror, your office cubicle—if safe to do so). Look at them several times a day for as many weeks or months as it takes for the truth in them to sink in.

---

Learning to separate who you are from what you do is essential if you are to find wholeness and balance in your life. Work, because it consumes so much time and energy in most of our lives, is a wonderful opportunity for making this discovery. Then, as you get clearer about who you are, about your needs and values, and about what matters most to you, you'll have more insight into the kind of work you really want to do.

## LOVING WHAT YOU DO

If you do what you love, the money may not necessarily immediately follow, but you can be sure of one thing—you'll be fulfilled. If you have to, you'll take a job that will give you the money you need to survive.

As just about every artist, writer, actor, and musician knows, you often have to work at a job you don't particularly like in order to pay the rent. Just make sure you take time for your creative work, for doing what you love. That will give you the energy and inspiration to carry you through the mundane work.

Suffering is bearable when you have a clear direction in life. You can do work you don't particularly enjoy if you know that it is leading toward something you really do want. Embracing the so-called bad in order to get to the good is sometimes necessary before you can find the balance you seek in life.

When work is done with presence, attention, and love, it becomes true service. It doesn't matter how menial, repetitive, or low-paying the job is, either. Marc Grossman, a teacher I once worked with, felt that all jobs, no matter what they are, have a twenty percent boredom, or drudge, factor. The level of your maturity, in his view, was in your ability to deal with it—to have the discipline to stick with what needs to be done. It's about follow-through, completion.

A number of the insights in this and the next two sections, on impeccability, and presence and focus, came out of my work with Marc. He reminded me, for instance, that luck is the residue of hard work. There's a powerful truth in that little statement. It's tempting at times to throw up our hands in disgust at what we consider to be our "bad" luck, but the wisest people know that we tend to make our own luck.

The more you put yourself into your life and work, the more you throw yourself into whatever it is you're doing, the more the gods, so to speak, are with you. It's amazing what can happen then. There's an inspiring quote from W. N. Murray, author of *The Scottish Himalayan Expedition,* which speaks to this:

"Until one is committed there is hesitancy, the chance to draw back, always ineffectiveness. Concerning all acts of initiative (and creation) there is one elementary truth, the ignorance of which kills countless ideas and splendid plans: the moment one definitely commits oneself, then Providence moves, too."

There's a strong connection between what we call "luck" and synchronicity, those meaningful "coincidences" that remind us of the magic and charm of life. In fact, I can give you a perfect example of synchronicity that happened just now, as I was writing this very section. I was thinking of the quote I just shared with you, but I didn't have it anywhere on file and I couldn't remember the exact words.

I paused in my work to see if I could find it in *Bartlett's Familiar Quotations* (it's not there), and then suddenly the phone rang. It was my friend Liz. We chatted, and I told her what I was working on, and asked her if she knew the quote.

"It's right here on my refrigerator!" she said.

"That proves my point!" I said jubilantly. "This is just what I'm writing about. When you throw yourself into your work, the universe moves to support you!"

If ever you find yourself complaining about your work, you're getting into your head and cutting yourself off from the now moment. Breathe, feel yourself in your body, come back to the task at hand. See if you can make the situation work for you. Take charge of it. Don't let it control you.

You know you're becoming free when, instead of complaining about your problems, you start being thankful for them. Again, this is where the Balancing Perceptions tool can be so effective. When you don't like what's happening, when you are faced with an upsetting problem or difficulty at work (or in any other area of your life), always remember to ask yourself, "So, there has to be something to learn from this. What's the gift here, the blessing? How is this serving my growth—even though it may not look like it from the outside?"

Remember, balancing your perceptions in this way is not "positive thinking." You are probing for the positive only to bring balance to your previously negative—and lopsided— view. Once you are able to see both sides clearly, both ways of looking at the problem, the negatives and positives neutralize each other, and you jump to a whole new level of awareness— one that is beyond thought altogether. You then tap into a powerful new current of energy and creativity, and the solution to the problem is generated out of that.

If there really is something you don't like about your work—or any other situation—find a way to change it. It's amazing what you can change when you set your mind to it. Above all, don't complain. Complaining only reinforces the feeling that you're a victim. It disempowers you.

The feeling of being a victim arises from taking things far too personally, and then holding on to the hurt feelings that result from believing you've been treated unfairly, or that the world is out to get you, or that you just don't have what it takes.

Remember, you are not your thoughts, beliefs, emotions, or circumstances. You are a powerful spiritual being, and at any time, you can choose to take a different action. If there's nothing you can do at the present moment to change a particular situation, let go of focusing on it and come back to the clarity and truth within you.

Come back to the peace and wholeness within you. Come back to that place of centeredness and balance within. This is always the best way to find balance and success in your work and outer life. Start from within, and then move out from there.

A friend, Peter, went through a major shift when he realized how much of a victim he felt in his job as a software consultant with a firm that did the payroll for a variety of small and medium-sized corporations.

I knew Peter's story well. He'd told it to me many times. (That's what victims do. They keep telling their "story," to the point where their friends sometimes get sick of hearing it. As you get free, you become less and less interested in the "story" of your own life.)

Peter was bright, smart, and knew he had more to contribute than many of the people he worked with who didn't really care about the job, but were there just for the money and the security. But he felt stuck because his supervisor, who was trying to hang on to his own position, was forever leaning on him. He was afraid that Peter's talents would make him look bad, and he resented him. And, Peter, of course, resented his supervisor.

When I spoke with Peter I brought up the subject of victimhood, and how it was, in my view, *the* ultimate disempowering attitude. I gently confronted him with the suggestion that maybe this was something he should look at. The beauty of a deep and valued friendship is that you're able to speak the truth in this way with each other. Indeed, you want the truth from each other.

"There are people in the world, mainly abused children and other innocents, who can legitimately be called 'victims,' " I said, "but most of us don't fall into that category. My own feelings of victimhood, while not major, were around the theme of how unfair life is, and why wasn't I born to wealthy parents . . . that kind of thing."

"How did you get beyond it?" Peter asked me.

"I just had to face the fact that my life wasn't working in certain areas, and it was precisely because I was holding on to those victimlike feelings. And, as K. used to say"—we were both, at one time, really into Krishnamurti—"the perception of truth brings its own action. It finally hit me between the eyes that being a victim just didn't *work*. So I dropped it. I stopped blaming God and other people for my situation, and took responsibility for my own life."

"And now?"

"When you no longer feel a victim of anything or anyone, there's an incredible feeling of freedom, of infinite possibility. It's *very* empowering."

A month later, Peter called me. There was a new energy in his voice. I could tell he'd made a breakthrough. "It's astounding how things have shifted," he said. "The people at the office, including my supervisor, are listening to me now, and giving my work the kind of serious attention I never got from them before."

"So what made the difference?"

He chuckled. "You know damned well what made the difference. I meditated on our conversation long and deep, and I finally realized how much of a victim I'd been. The 'poor me' syndrome."

He paused. "So I just let go of it. I let go of the resentment. I let go of the story. I let go of the attachment to results, and to what they thought of me. I decided to just do my job as well as I could, and leave the rest up to the universe. It was like letting go of a tremendous burden. I feel the best, in terms of my energy and confidence, that I've felt in years."

I congratulated him. "It's going to make a big difference in the life of your son and daughter, too."

"Yes," he agreed, "It's good to break that cycle of victimhood. I don't want them growing up with that attitude."

Peter's internal shift was a great example of how we can positively influence not just our children but anyone with whom we live or work. By being as clear and conscious as we can be, and by taking full responsibility for our own circumstances, we inspire those around us. In this way the world is changed, one person at a time.

## IMPECCABILITY

To do really good work is to be impeccable. It's to act flawlessly, to be as close to perfect, in the sense of no errors or ragged edges, as it is humanly possible to be.

At the same time, it's important not to judge yourself when you fall short of your chosen mark. People cut off their creativity and potential by being too hard on themselves. The realization that I wanted to strive for perfection in my work, but that *I* didn't need to be perfect—especially not "perfectly" en-lightened—was one of the great liberating discoveries of my life.

Part of being impeccable is staying on top of things. It's be-ing "squared away." It's ensuring that you complete the tasks and projects you take on. Unfinished business is an energy drain. The more you procrastinate with those projects and messy situations that you know you should be attending to, the more the thought of them eats away at you. Shit stinks, but it stinks worse if you don't clean it up!

I used to watch how a friend, Phil, carefully cleaned and oiled his lawn mower every time he finished cutting his grass. He'd put it away in its proper place in the garage, and it would be clean and sparkling, ready to do a perfect job the next time. At the end of every year, Phil works overtime to complete ev-erything that is still undone, both in his business and around his house. That way he gets to start the new year with a clean slate. Not a bad practice at all!

Impeccability is the mark of the spiritual warrior. To find balance in the world of work, business, and the marketplace, you must be able to draw on the warrior energy within. When-ever the outer situation looks like it might be spinning out of control or threatening your well-being in some other way, it's time to consciously do your centering and grounding exercises. You have to pause, breathe, and come back to that place of clar-ity and strength within.

Successful work requires will and discipline. These are not ego traits but expressions of your real nature. The way to de-velop a strong will and good discipline is through learning to trust yourself. This means accepting your feelings, emotions, impulses, your shadow side. When you deny any part of your-self, it causes conflict within you, a lack of congruency, or wholeness, and this just weakens your will.

As Marc Grossman says, every job is a self-portrait of the person who performed it. I would add that it's important not to become infatuated with your own picture! In other words, take the job seriously, but not yourself. The best work is always when there is no trace of "you" in it. Keep your ego out of it, and your work will go well.

You've got to know how to walk in balance in the world. People create stress for themselves because they get overextended in one direction or another. They lose the balance. The farther out you get, the harder it is to come back. Stay close to the center!

Here's another piece of wisdom that came through in my work with Marc: when considering embarking on any new venture with someone, ask yourself, "Would I climb a mountain with this person? Are they strong enough to save me if I fall? Are they strong enough not to fall so that I don't have to worry constantly about saving them?" If you can't answer yes to all three questions, find a new climbing partner!

Partnerships in work and business are no different than marriages. When trust isn't there, or you don't share the same vision, or are not putting in equal effort and energy, or the communication breaks down, the partnership fails. And getting a divorce from a business partner is no less costly, both financially and emotionally, than separating from a spouse. Be very clear, then, about the work and business commitments you make.

The following exercise came out of my work with Marc. If you want to be on top of your work and perform at the highest possible level with the least amount of stress, I recommend you do this exercise every three months for a year. Impeccability is one of the secrets for finding the balance between your inner spiritual well-being and success in the world of the marketplace.

## TOOL #14
## IMPECCABILITY CHECKLIST

The first part of this exercise is to write down the names of three people who are your models for excellence, for impeccability. These are people who embody, in your view, a high degree of inner clarity and serenity, balanced with outer focus and productivity. Ask yourself the following questions with regard to each person. Write down your answers. Meditate on them. Take action if appropriate:

What can I most learn from this person? What specific questions do I have for him or her? Would I benefit from spending more time with this person? Can I find a way to do that? How might I be able to help them? (Speak to them and find out.)

For the second part of the exercise, review the quality of the work you do and your relationship with it by grading yourself as you answer the following questions (4 = always, 3 = often, 2 = seldom, 1 = never):

1. Do I give my work my total attention?

2. Do I work with humility, a willingness to let others take credit?

3. Do I respect my coworkers, their methods, and their philosophies?

4. Do I have the attitude that everyone is a guru, a wise person in disguise?

5. Will my actions stand up to scrutiny and to the inevitable stresses of life?

6. Is it my full and total effort?

7. Have I attended to all the details?

8. Have I acted with patience and presence?

9. Do I add value to my work by going the extra mile and giving more than is expected?

10. Am I unattached to the outcome of my efforts?

If you score 25 or less, you've got a lot of work to do yet on yourself. You're probably under too much stress, and your life is definitely out of balance. Some good guidance in the form of mentoring or coaching will help. A score of 26–35 means you're not drowning, but you could certainly benefit from guidance. Above 35 indicates that you are committed to your work and your life, and you have a healthy balance between your inner well-being and your outer success. You are probably a role model for others, whether you know it or not.

---

Successful work is about breaking through the barriers and taking full responsibility for your life. What if you jumped into your life? Do it. Give it everything you've got. You won't regret it.

As long as you can say you did your best and have no doubts about it, then you have acted impeccably.

## PRESENCE AND FOCUS

To be impeccable in your work is to be wholly present in it. It's to realize, at the same time, that you are responsible for your efforts, not for the results. Understand the simple truth of this, and non-attachment to outcomes—the ultimate position of freedom—becomes easy.

You can certainly *intend* a result, and much of the time you'll get the result you want. But if you put too much emphasis on controlling the outcome of everything that happens, it means your ego is heavily tied up in the process. When things turn out the way you want, the tendency is to feel an inflated sense of pride and accomplishment. When things don't go your way, you risk becoming emotionally stressed, undone, even depressed.

Look at people you know who fall into the category of "control-freaks." They invariably live with a high degree of tension and stress. While a certain amount of control energy is needed to succeed in business, especially if you're an entrepreneur, the stress-free path lies in finding the balance between control and surrender, between the dance of grace and will.

The Bhagavad Gita, the Hindu holy book, instructs the student of conscious living to "Act, but don't be attached to the fruits of your actions." Not to be attached to the results of your work frees you up to be fully present *with* your work.

Have you noticed that very often you have to really get into a creative project and spend time with it before you know where it's going? Writers, artists, and musicians know this. It's what it means to be "guided" by the work itself. When I write, for instance, I start out with a very clear idea of where I'm going.

I see the mountaintop, if you like, and I aim for it. But I don't always have a clear idea of how I'm going to get there. It would spoil the fun and limit the creative opportunities if I had every step of the way planned. Besides, once I get started on the writing journey, I often find myself being inexorably pulled in another direction, toward a mountain I hadn't even noticed before.

For true creativity, there can be no formula or code to follow. When I jump into the day's writing, new ideas, insights, and possibilities start jumping right back at me, both from the computer monitor and out of my brain. It makes for fun, exciting, *original* work, when you're never quite sure what's going to come forth!

This is one of the differences between a novice and a master. A novice tries to make the work happen, but a master gives shape to it as it unfolds. Learn to give shape to your life and your work as it unfolds, instead of trying to control every event and outcome, and you'll start dancing in the delightful and magical realm of mastery. Then you'll truly enjoy your work.

Like relationships, work is a test of how well you're learning life's lessons. Most people struggle with different aspects of the curriculum—and not without a price. As Phil, the friend I quoted earlier, says, the school of hard knocks exacts a very high tuition.

Part of the learning is to be clear about what you're going to focus on, and then get focused. A person who chases two rabbits ends up catching neither. Or, in the words of a Zen master: "Sit or stand, above all, don't wobble." Choose a direction, a course of action, and zero in on it.

You access extraordinary power when you take a stand. It doesn't matter if it turns out to be the wrong stand, either. The universe is quick to provide feedback to committed people—and just as quick in giving you the opportunity to choose again, should you make a mistake.

When I was young and training to be an army officer, one of our sergeant instructors used to say, "If you're going to make a mistake, make it a bold one." Excellent advice, and the surest way to eliminate time-wasting, wishy-washy, pussyfooting around. Besides, the more you know yourself and the more grounded you are in the truth of your own being, the more you realize that there are no real mistakes, only lessons.

There are some opportunities that come around only once or twice in a lifetime. These are the "windows" that can launch you into a totally new direction, or a higher level of participation. It takes wisdom to recognize them—and courage to accept the invitation. Timing is everything. If it's not the right time, it's not going to happen. Be patient. Your time will come.

There's no growth, no transformation, without risk. If you want to have your work be all it can be, let go of worrying about outcomes and plunge into the creative process itself. And re-member—work flows best and most fruitfully when you do it from a desire to *give*, rather than get.

## PASSION AND SECURITY

Passion and security tend to be mutually exclusive terms. To pursue your passion is to risk throwing security to the winds. To focus first and foremost on security, especially of the mate-rial kind, often means that you sacrifice your passion.

Too many people give up their dreams for the sake of secu-rity. Their fear causes them to close down, to opt for the com-fort and safety of the known, rather than risking the road less-traveled. The irony is that, later in life, much of their fi-nancial security is often expended on medical bills, on trying to arrest the physical degeneration that is the all-too-frequent product of a chronically unfulfilled and unhappy life. Don't let this happen to you.

To follow the herd is to end up traveling a relatively clear, safe, and uneventful path through life. If you strike out on your own, you'll inevitably encounter thorns and obstacles—but you'll arrive at a place that is truly yours. It's up to you. There's no right or wrong. It's just a question of how passion-ately, how adventurously, you want to live. And what you want to be able to look back on, when you reach the end of a partic-ular road.

To find the balance you seek in your life, it's sometimes necessary to push the envelope, to go out on a limb, before you can come back to a truer center, to a place that feels more "you."

Jack London wrote, "I would rather be a superb meteor, every atom of me in magnificent glow, than a sleepy and permanent planet. The proper function of man is to live, not to exist. I shall not waste my days in trying to prolong them. I shall use my time."

Security is never guaranteed, anyway. You never know whether your next breath is going to be your last. Breathe deep. Plunge in. After all, there's no failure, only lessons—some of them hard at times. But the more you risk and the more you learn what you're supposed to learn, the easier the lessons get. The more you know yourself at a deep, spiritual level, the easier it is to find the balance between a life passionately lived and your needs around material security.

The words of Carlos Castaneda's teacher, Don Juan, are a useful reminder here: "The true warrior takes calculated risks." Only a fool rushes in blindly, but there comes a time, a point of transition, when you must make a move, a choice. If you don't choose, life will choose for you. As you follow your dreams and let your passion take fire, you don't have to burn all your bridges. You don't have to give everything up in the material realm.

It's the letting go of the *attachment* that is the key. You find your well-being within, from awakening to the beauty, mystery, and power of your spirit, and then you no longer need to worry about how secure your job is, or how much money you have in the bank, or what will happen next week.

You start to develop a deep, innate trust for the natural unfolding of life. You realize that the universe, this earth, really is an abundant place, and your needs will *always* be met. This is the fundamental realization about the material realm that all enlightened people come to. They absolutely know and trust that life will always, one hundred percent of the time, take care of them. They may not know *how,* but they know it will.

Do work that ignites your passion and gives you the opportunity to contribute to the well-being of others, and security won't be a problem. You'll be filled with love and gratitude for the opportunity to serve, and it will come back to you a thousand times.

But you must give unconditionally for this to happen. You can't do it with the *expectation* of a particular result. This is why you must let go of attachment to outcomes. This is why you must know yourself, why you must be truly free within—for how else will you find the courage to let go?

So, when you work, focus on the quality of your actions— your contribution—not on the results. The joy is always in the journey, the creating. Remember this. Then you won't have to worry about security or how things are going to turn out.

## SUCCESS

In its simplest definition, success is simply achieving your goals, doing what makes you happy. To resent another's success is to push success away from you. To welcome another's success is to draw it to you. Start being happy for those who are succeeding, and one day you'll succeed yourself.

Success is a natural by-product when you're passionate about your work. To *want* to succeed at what you do is the first criterion for success. If you want to succeed at the highest level possible, your work must be of the highest quality. Sometimes, the only difference between success and failure is the degree to which you've taken care of the details. Don't settle for anything less than your absolute best.

If you just want to slide by in life, you may well be able to pull it off. But when you slide by, you also slip through. You slip through the cracks, and your work doesn't get noticed. Wasted potential is one of the great tragedies in life. Don't waste yours.

It's a tough world out there, but remember this: no one can compete with you when you're being yourself. No one can say what you have to say, or do what you have to do, as well as you can. That sounds obvious, but whenever you fall into self-doubt, it's worth remembering. I know my life got a whole lot easier when I stopped trying to be somebody I wasn't.

When I was traveling in India in 1983, I was staying, at one point, in a cheap hotel in the cantonment section of Varanasi, or Benares, which sits on the banks of the Ganges and is the holiest—and oldest—city in India. I remember waking one morning, getting some deliciously hot *chai* from the front desk, and going up onto the rooftop patio.

As I drank my tea in the early-morning sun, I looked down on the street below and watched India coming alive. There was a park, ringed by aging banyan trees, and on the other side of it was a dilapidated-looking YMCA. Several crows flew lazily by overhead, cawing as they passed. A man rolled up with a cart, which he was setting up as a little outdoor barber shop. A couple of cows wandered by. Some kids were playing. Two old ladies in faded saris squatted in the shade of one of the banyan trees, and began chattering away with each other.

I breathed in the fragrance, the pungent smells, of India. Ah, it felt so good to be there, away from the busyness of the life I had left behind in California. I felt so alive, so free! What a joy to travel in a country like India, where the spiritual energy was so strong it seemed that you could feel the presence of God everywhere.

Standing on that rooftop, basking in my freedom, I thought of Paul, a friend back in California, a very successful business-man whose life revolved around doing deals and making money. How good it felt not to have him asking me how much money I had grossed in the month since we had last talked! How good it felt to be away from America, with its endless emphasis on production, consumption, and the almighty dollar! How good it felt to just *be,* to be free to be myself, unconstrained by all that materialistic, competitive energy!

Discover *your* truth, and commit your life to that. That's what India taught me. That's what it means to follow your bliss. Commitment is power. When you make a commitment to something, you draw—as the Murray quote earlier demonstrates—unseen energies and forces in support of your efforts. This is how the universe works. It gives you back exactly what you put out. Put out mixed messages, and you'll get mixed results. Be clear about what you want, and you'll get that.

Find your voice, then *use* it. Sing your song. People are waiting to hear it. Listen, at the same time, for how you are being received. Feedback is essential for learning—it's how you know how well you're doing. If the feedback you're getting bothers you, then you've definitely got something to learn. The universe, in the form of other people, is telling you you need to do something differently (or maybe you just need to let go of worrying about other people's judgments).

One thing you can be sure of: when you put yourself out there, people *will* judge you. Learn from their judgments if there is learning to be had, but don't take them personally. Don't let what others say about you become yet another "story" to cover up the light of your own inner wisdom and power.

Persistence is important for success. Consider the motto of my junior high school: "Effort, perseverance, success." But to have the best chance of winning, you must also learn the rules of the game being played. Business has its rules, successful work has its rules, just as there are rules for successful relationships, and for getting enlightened.

The practical part of this book is about the rules. Learn them. Discover them. Heck, make your own, if you can get them to work for you—if you can get others to agree, and to play your game.

And remember: success always comes, eventually, to those who stay the course. Don't be a quitter. At the same time, don't be so stuck that you can't change direction when needed.

## GOALS

To accomplish anything successfully in the material universe, you must have a goal, an intent. Otherwise, you're like a cork bobbing helplessly about on the ocean of life. You're just floating aimlessly.

Sometimes, however, to roam aimlessly about is not only fun but it's also the exact thing you need to be doing at a particular time in your life—opening yourself to the unknown. But it's also necessary, much of the time, to have a clear course in front of you, to know your general direction. It's the balance, once again.

Worldly problems become less bothersome when you have a meaningful goal you're pursuing. Keep your eye on the goal, and somehow the problems will work themselves out. They always do. If you don't have a goal to focus your energies on, your energy gets scattered, and all you can see are problems. They can quickly become overwhelming, and in their wake come the dreaded specters of defeat and failure.

No matter what your work is, if you want to succeed at it you've got to believe in yourself. If you don't believe in you, who will? Disappointment and rejection are facts of life. The more deeply you know yourself at a spiritual level, the less you take rejection personally. Your commitment to your work, your path, is so strong that you will let nothing deter you.

You intuitively grasp the relevance and meaning of the line from the Bhagavad Gita that says, "It is better to fail at your own *dharma*—your own mission in life—than to succeed at another person's." After all, it's not success for its own sake that you seek. That's the fantasy of people who feel empty, who feel that they are not enough inside themselves. No, you have a destiny to fulfill, a unique or particular piece of work that you want to accomplish, and give to the world.

Successful people have learned to stay focused on their goals, their objectives, and not get sidetracked by the inevitable obstacles and complications that crop up along the way.

Learn from those who are successful, but don't rush to emulate them. You waste energy and incur frustration chasing someone else's goals. I've seen people make this mistake a lot, especially when they are trying to "model" someone they admire, someone who is very successful. By all means, learn from others about what it takes to succeed, but don't try and be a clone of someone else. You can only succeed in life when you are being yourself. Set goals that light a fire in your heart.

Goals that are pursued as a compensation for feeling empty never satisfy for long. The emptiness soon looms again. Find out who you are. Work on embodying the core insight, the clarity and fullness of your true nature. Then listen for the creative passion that wants to emerge from within you, and let your goals be an outgrowth of that. As you get in touch with your real values and needs, the work you're meant to be doing becomes clearer to you.

When you know what you're here to do, you've found your purpose in life. Then you can develop goals that are in alignment with your purpose. They become way stations on the road to fulfilling your purpose. When considering your purpose and goals, ask yourself, "What have I always dreamed of doing?" Then find a way to begin doing it.

Getting clear about the goals that matter to you, and then writing them down, is valuable. You set an intention that, if you pursue it to the end, will lead you to the achievement of your goals. As one of my favorite fortune cookies says, "If you can shape it in your mind, you will find it in your life." The following tool will help clarify and prioritize your goals.

## TOOL #15
## PRIORITIZING GOALS

Begin, as with most of these exercises, by breathing, relaxing, and centering yourself. This particular tool can be used either to clarify your goals or to review the ones you have. It is a very simple process. Just ask yourself the following questions, think long and hard about your responses, and then write them down.

1. If I could accomplish only one work or creative goal in my life, what would that be?

It might be to become an executive in your corporation, build a successful business as an entrepreneur, develop a new product, revolutionize an industry, write a book, direct a movie, or simply find a job or work you really love.

After settling on the most important one, choose several other goals you'd like to accomplish. The value of choosing one primary goal—the "what if this was the only thing I ever got to do?" goal—is that it gets you very, very focused. And to achieve a high level of success at anything in life, the ability to focus in a single-minded way is essential. Every high-achiever has developed this skill.

Always remember, however, that focus and single-mindedness, while powerful and extremely useful *functions,* are not the be-all and end-all of existence. For a truly balanced and happy life, you must be able to let go of the intense focus and balance it with enjoyment of the creative process and the ability to just delight in the moment. That's why the next question is important.

2. If I could accomplish only one spiritual goal in my life, what would that be?

Perhaps you might answer, "Why, to learn how to *relax* and be." Or maybe you'd express it as something like inner peace, knowing God, enlightenment, unconditional love, compassion—or, if you're really getting the message of this book, "embodying the core insight and becoming inwardly free."

Then do the same question-and-answer process for each of the following life areas: Health, relationship, creativity, contribution to others or to the world . . . and any other areas that are important to you. (You can focus on your financial goals in this exercise, or wait till the next chapter.)

The final part of this exercise is to select the top three goals from all of the above. If God spoke to you and said you could accomplish only three of your major goals in this lifetime, what would they be? Get clear about that question, and then begin paying attention to what you do with your energy each day. Are you staying focused on your goals? Are you using your energy in a way that supports the attainment of them? Are your daily actions congruent with who you are and what you say you're about?

———————————————————————

Once you know your goals, put them at the back of your mind and concentrate on the journey. When you feel yourself getting off track, review your goals. They'll remind you of where you're heading. Meditate on them. Visualize them happening in reality—actually see, feel, touch, taste, and smell what it would be like if the goal were accomplished.

Intention is your aim, the goal is what is aimed for. Clarifying your goals focuses your intention. The more real the goal becomes—through your power to visualize, sense, feel, and imagine it—the clearer your intention. Soon, intention and goal become one. What was previously only a vision is now reality.

Finally, when it seems like you might never achieve the goal that has mattered so much to you, that you've been working so hard toward, remember this: when the thing you want most seems farthest away, that is often the time you're about to get it. The last half mile of any journey is usually the hardest.

Renew your commitment to the process, the work at hand, completely release attachment to the outcome, and be ready to be surprised.

## HOW TO ATTRACT WHAT YOU WANT

Getting clear about what you really want helps draw the desired object to you. This is the law of attraction at work. Clarity is power. When your intention is clear and you have no emotional attachment to the outcome, things manifest very quickly.

When your goal and intention are unclear, you're forever reaching out, trying to grasp at an ill-defined and elusive target. You find yourself pushing to make something happen. You waste a lot of energy.

When you push, energy spins off in all directions. Think of trying to push an apple across a flat surface, and how difficult it is to control its movements. Now visualize pulling that same apple toward you with an imaginary string. It moves in a straight line. Pulling is the most efficient use of energy.

Or think of it this way: when you're always "pushing" to make something happen in your life, you're literally trying to manipulate, or shape, forces and energies outside yourself. You're trying to mold these forces—events, other people—to fit your agenda. You're trying to get the outer energy to do what you want it to do.

But have you ever noticed that events, other people, and outside forces have an energy, a will, of their own? It's not that you can't succeed in pushing and shaping the world around you to conform to your wishes, but it requires a tremendous amount of focus, will, effort, and—usually—struggle. It can leave you exhausted. Plus it makes other people resent you, especially if they feel they are being manipulated.

Learning to *pull* the desired object to you, however, is a whole different game. It's what true masters in any field do. The way to do it is to get very centered in your body, in your own power, through being supremely aware and present. When you do this, you're literally pulling energy in from the universe around you. You're gathering energy, rather than dissipating it.

There's a simple experiment you can do to test this. The next time you go to a bar, restaurant, or social gathering, get dressed up in really attractive clothes. Sit in your car and meditate before you go into the establishment. Get centered. Then, when you walk in, feel yourself being very grounded in and connected to your body.

Walk smoothly, gracefully, naturally. Be totally in the moment. Be completely cool. Be aware of the people around you, but in an unconditional way. Simply project what is true: you are a human being fully at ease with yourself, completely juiced on the energy you feel inside your own being. And then just notice how many looks you attract, from people of both sexes!

Men, with their egocentric power needs, tend to push. Women, with traditionally less outer power at their disposal, have thousands of years of training in how to attract, pull in, what they want. Men can learn a lot from watching how women operate in the world. The secret is to be very *clear* about what you want, put your intention out there, then let go of any attachment to it. Then it can come to you.

It's the same with solving problems. The shortest, simplest, and most intelligent way to find the solution to any problem in your work—or any other area of your life, including health, relationships, and money—is to give the problem more attention. Remember, energy flows where attention goes.

So, focus on the problem. This intensifies the problem, amplifies it. As it grows in your awareness, it'll reveal new things to you—including, eventually, its own solution. But there's a caveat here. When you amplify the problem, when you turn up the heat, so to speak, things can get intense and uncomfortable—which is precisely why a lot of problems don't get solved. A lot of people would prefer to live in denial. They pretend the problem doesn't exist.

But just as the problem is always here, so is the solution, awaiting your attention. The solution is always in the problem itself. You just have to get outside the problem (realize that you're bigger than it) through expanding your awareness, through getting some detachment. Then zero in with your attention. Really focus on the situation—and breathe through any discomfort it brings up. Focused attention will attract, draw to you, insights and opportunities that were previously hidden. This is guaranteed.

And remember this: as long as you're alive there will always be problems. The clearer and freer you are inside, however, the less problematic they will be.

### *POWER*

Work is power made manifest. Business authors Warren Bennis and Burt Nanus define power as the ability to translate intention into reality. The more powerful you are, I've observed, the more quickly it happens.

Powerful people have very clear intention, and very focused attention. They realize the importance of balancing perception, intention, and energy expenditure.

Knowledge without power is ineffectual, and power without knowledge is dangerous. For work to be productive, meaningful, and of value to all affected by it, knowledge and power have to fuse—and the fusion point is in the heart. When knowledge and power meet in the heart, the result is true wisdom.

Authentic power is to live in your body, from your heart, with your intention focused on serving the greater good. When you let your own needs be secondary, everything begins to happen for you.

Love is the key to authentic power, to the right use of will. Let your work be a labor of love. There's fundamentally only one power, one energy in life, but there are two ways you can access it—through the ego or through the heart.

Ego power relies on personal will, force, domination—the compulsive urge to manipulate and control others. It's a destructive power. It divides the world into "you" and "me," into "us" and "them." Ego power, in order to build and maintain itself, depends upon the control and disempowerment of others. This kind of power poisons work for all who are involved in it. The only "good" thing about it is that, in the end, it always self-destructs. Dictators, tyrants, and false prophets always, sooner or later, fall.

Power, which is the life force, the human spirit, is an awesome and inexhaustible river of energy. It will eventually annihilate anyone who tries to dam the flow of it or hoard it for themselves.

Healthy power is a function of somatic integrity—of being relaxed yet alert in body, mind, and spirit. When you are really present in your work, you are in your body. You are using power in a healthy way when, instead of just trying to master the moment, you become interested in sensing and feeling it, in having a *relationship* with it. Feeling leads to mastery, not the other way around.

For power to express itself constructively, it needs a vehicle. The vehicle takes shape in the kind of work you do, the cause you get behind, the project you're committed to completing.

Authentic power is always shared. It serves a larger purpose than just taking care of your own needs. As you get freer of self-interest and the kind of overweening personal ambition that is the sign of ego-centered living, more creative energy becomes available to you than you could ever have imagined. When this energy is harnessed in the service of others, your own needs are more than amply provided for.

When you live from your heart, you become a conduit for the power of love. This power then flows out to serve and to heal others. It is continually self-renewing. The qualities of the heart are humility, non-judgment, affection, trust, and generosity.

The heart is the great balancer in work and in life. If ever you feel conflict between what you're thinking and what you're feeling, between what's happening outside you and your internal reaction to it, come back to your heart. Breathe, feel your feet on the ground, sense your body, listen to your heart.

Find a way to use your work as a vehicle for giving love to people, for really connecting with them at a heart level, and you'll always be happy and successful at what you do.

## SPIRITUALITY IN THE CORPORATE WORLD

When you work for yourself, you have a lot of freedom to create a nourishing, supportive work environment. But if you work for a corporation, you may well find yourself sitting with the question: How can I be an authentic human being, how can

I really be *me,* while I'm working for an organization with a primary focus on productivity, results, and the bottom line, and an organizational culture that disregards my spiritual values?

If this is a question that drives you, that is a source of stress for you—and it is a common complaint, or dilemma, in the corporate world—the best way of solving it is to literally live with the question. Make it your personal mission to find that sense of wholeness and authenticity within even as you fulfill your corporate responsibilities.

As you do this, as you open up more fully to the core insight, the knowledge of who and what you are beyond all your beliefs, beyond the story that has run your life up till now, you'll stop looking to your work, and the corporate culture itself, for identity and meaning. Your essential well-being will no longer depend on the corporation. It will no longer depend on whether you even have a job or not; it will come increasingly from the beauty and power of the life force moving through you.

While you're still in the process of discovering this inner freedom, however, there are steps you can take to make your experience of going to work each day much more nourishing at a personal level.

First of all, remind yourself daily of what is fundamentally true about the rules of the corporate game—it's about winning, making a profit. It has to be this way, because if a corporation—like any business entity—doesn't make a profit, it doesn't get to stay around.

The unfortunate by-product of this "rule" is that, at the highest level, corporate executives—like most people who are very materialistic in their orientation—tend to operate mainly from ego. And if you don't yet understand this fact about the ego, you will soon: the overriding concern of the ego, the personal self, is its own survival, and thus its chief operating emotion is fear.

In an interview published in the business magazine *Fast Company,* an Intel vice-president said, "There are two things that run our industry: paranoia and greed. We go back and forth between the two . . . but paranoia is the more effective one." Interestingly, this man's boss, Andy Grove, the CEO of Intel, titled his recent biography *Only The Paranoid Survive.*

A consultant friend of mine supports this view. "The fear factor is huge," she says, "and it's not only because the competition is so ferocious. 'Watch your ass' becomes the governing mantra just for survival in your own job. After all, anything you might say can be used against you. Tell your boss the truth, and you risk getting fired."

Another friend, who recently got laid off from an upper-level management position at a major Silicon Valley firm, reminded me that there are real things to be afraid of in the corporate world. "Our lives can be gone in a second. How could we not have fear? Look what happened to me. Fear is one of the greatest motivators not only to do the best job possible, but to say or do whatever it takes to hold on to that job."

What made the transition from job to no job easier for this particular friend—besides the fact that she had no family or mortgage to worry about—was her deep grounding in her spirituality. She had for some years viewed her life as a spiritual journey. She made a daily practice of using the tools of centering, breathing, grounding, and remembering to be aware.

You can do this, too. Throughout the day, while you're at work, pause every hour or so and take a minute or two just to disconnect from the spin, the whirlwind of activity being generated around you, and come back to your*self.* Breathe, feel yourself in your body, be still, come fully into the moment. Tune in to the deeper, calmer energy that is always here underneath the surface chaos and stress. Then, from that place of present-time awareness, consciously move into action with your next task or project.

If you need help to remind you to do this, place a small sign somewhere in your workspace, a sign that says something like "Breathe! "Remember, I *have* work, but I am *not* my work," "Work goes best when I keep myself out of the way," or "Be here now." Some people like to set the beeper on their digital watch to go off every hour as a reminder.

The support of others makes a huge difference, too. Feel out fellow workers who are interested in a more conscious and stress-free work environment. Get together with them at lunch or other breaks. Discuss the books you're reading—like this one—and the progress you're making on your path of growth and transformation. Brainstorm what you can do to create a more supportive climate for the heart/spirit connection at work, and for a more honest and compassionate dialogue between management and employees.

At Mount Madonna Center in the Santa Cruz mountains of California there is a yoga community founded by Baba Hari Das, a famous yogi who has been in silence for more than thirty years. He communicates his pithy wisdom by writing on a chalkboard. Every summer the community has its own "Olympics," and there is a large banner that hangs near the volleyball court, with one of Baba Hari Das's sayings on it: "Play for fun, die to win!"

Play for fun, die to win. A great motto for life, and especially for the corporate game, and for the game of work in general. To play for fun means you're in it for the enjoyment, the process, the shared experience with others on your team, and not just for the final reward. This attitude alone will eliminate seventy-five percent of the stress you feel at work—and the remaining twenty-five percent you can learn how to handle.

Die to win means that you give it your all. You're one hundred percent there. You play your heart out. You do everything humanly possible to ensure the desired outcome, but your emotional and spiritual well-being are not tied to the results. They come from within, direct expressions of your true nature, of who you are when "you," with all your ego-based considerations and concerns, are out of the way.

Learn to do that, keep learning it until it becomes second nature for you, and no matter how crazy, chaotic, or stressful things get at work, you will always be okay.

### CHAPTER SIX

# *Dealing with Money*

## *TRUE ABUNDANCE*

*I* figured out a long time ago that there were only two ways to be free of worry about money. One was to have so much of it that it didn't matter, and the other was to take the path of enlightenment and inwardly get free of worry *period,* so that whether you had money or not, your fundamental well-being was unaffected.

When I looked even more closely at these two options, I saw that, actually, there was really only one viable path for me, and that was the latter one. After all, I knew of many people with a lot of money, people who theoretically (if option number one was true) should no longer have any worries about money. Yet they still worried.

They worried about holding on to their money, and they were bent on making still more of it. I knew of people who had millions of dollars, and it still wasn't enough to assuage their fears of poverty, of not having enough. Maybe, with some of them, it was just greed, an addiction. Who knows? I just knew that if I took the first path, if I focused all my efforts on making money, no matter how much money I accumulated, it still wouldn't bring me the deep inner peace and happiness for which my soul cried out.

So I took the latter path—the road less traveled, you might say. But I still had a lot of lessons to learn about getting money in balance in my life, because in our culture—no matter what your creative or spiritual focus—not much can happen without it. And there's no doubt that the more money you have, the easier certain aspects of life are.

Let me give you some personal background. Since I was young, I have always had a strong connection to the spiritual, and it only got stronger after I went through the health crisis that, at age twenty-nine, started me on my real spiritual journey.

It happened when one night I suddenly found myself experiencing all the symptoms of what I thought was a heart attack, and for months I was afraid to go to sleep at night for fear I would die. Eventually I figured out it was stress, a chronic, underlying anxiety I had. I lived in my head, and was always pursuing some goal in the future. I began reading books on how to relax. I read books on spirituality and transformation. I took a course in meditation. I began doing yoga. I started to learn about living in the present. I soon became hooked on the whole idea of enlightenment, of inner peace and freedom.

My spiritual journey led me to the realization of the core insight that I'm sharing with you in this book. It led me to the freedom I had so long sought. But with the material dimension in life—specifically, money—it has been a different story. I didn't feel the same degree of ease or comfort in that realm. The challenges I've had around money in the past really tested my inner freedom.

I grew up in a lower-middle-class family in New Zealand. We not only never had much money but it also seemed I was raised with a consciousness of lack, of scarcity. My paternal grandmother, Mary Manson Dreaver, was the third woman elected to the Parliament in New Zealand. She was a member of the Labor party, a staunch socialist, and very committed to the principle of the welfare state and to working for women's rights. She was also a minister in the spiritualist church, the hostess of a national radio show, a teacher of pianoforte, an accomplished artist with oils, and the mother of six children—an amazing woman!

My grandmother's socialist, working-class values definitely affected me. I think I bought into the idea that money was "dirty," it wasn't quite okay, and those who had a lot of it had made it by exploiting the poor and downtrodden.

When you marry this semi-Marxist perspective with the kind of strong spiritual inclinations I had (and then add in the fact that I secretly hoped that someday I would be, if not rich, then at least affluent myself!) it's easy to understand why I might have had some confusion and guilt about money.

Eventually, it was the core insight that saved me and that resolved the confusion. When I finally came to the realization that I was not my story, my money problems, or any of the other circumstances in my life, I began to see my relationship with money in a whole new light.

Money, I saw, was just money. It was a tool, a very necessary and useful part of life. As I relinquished all my beliefs, judgments, and fears around it—including my socialist *and* capitalist tendencies—money ceased being a problem. I stopped worrying about money in the same way that I stopped worrying about everything else.

After all, "who" was worrying? When you no longer hold on to any image or concept of self, there's no persisting sense of self to get upset about things. There is just awareness, presence, the endless flow and fullness of *being*. And when something needs to be done, when the situation calls for action, you—as *aware-*

*ness,* as the conscious and creative being you are—jump into action. This is the core insight and, once you see it, it's so obvious that you find yourself thinking, "How come it took me so long to realize this?"

When I saw all this and stopped worrying, two things happened: first, it became easier to focus on my work and on making money without concern for how well I was going to do, and second, money began to flow into my life in a more effortless and abundant way.

"Seek ye first the kingdom of God," Jesus taught, "and all these things shall be added unto you." In other words, find that richness of spirit within, that deep and abiding feeling of love, inner peace, happiness, and well-being, and you'll walk in the world without fear. You'll do whatever you need to do to generate income, and it will come to you, because there will be nothing in your consciousness to block it.

This is the real meaning of abundance. It begins within, and until you've found the inner treasure, then no matter how much money you have, you'll always feel poor in spirit. You'll feel anxious and insecure inside. But once you've connected with the energy and creative power that is the very substance of your innermost being, then you'll always feel rich, whether you have money or not.

Now, doesn't that sound like a great way to live, a great space to be in? Come with me on this phase of the journey, then, as we explore the relationship between money and spirituality, and how to resolve any conflict between the two.

### THE FLOW OF MONEY

Money is one of the rewards for work well done. If you put out enough good, heartfelt energy in a focused and consistent way, so that it provides real value for people—that is, so that it gives people something they want, and are willing to pay money for—money will flow back to you. This is a fundamental law of the material universe.

Opening your heart, then, is very much one of the critical keys to financial prosperity, but this must be balanced with a clear understanding of what money is and how it works. The physical universe, remember, is governed by laws of cause and effect.

That's why the rich have so much money. They understand the second half of the equation; they have mastered the rules of the money game. However, don't perpetuate your own "story" around lack, of being chronically short of money, by falling into the trap of envying the rich. It's the *feeling* of being rich inside, rich in spirit, that counts first and foremost—and that has nothing to do with the size of your bank account. No amount of money can fill the hole in a person's soul.

If your spiritual well-being depends on how much money you have, you're not free. Believe it or not, this is where having too much money can actually be a disadvantage, a liability. It becomes too easy to insulate yourself from the harsher realities of life, to escape into diversion or distraction whenever you feel restless or bored.

You never have to really face yourself, in other words, because you have the financial wherewithal to escape to wherever you want, whenever the mood strikes you. And if you never have to face yourself, you're never going to tap into your true spiritual nature. So, you keep on escaping and compensating, and meanwhile your heart grows harder and harder, and you get farther and farther away from the truth and beauty that is your innermost spiritual nature.

However, to think that money is somehow unspiritual is also naive. It's a false and very limiting belief. As Gandhi said, you can't talk to a starving man about God. What he needs is bread. And to get bread, you must have—bread! The fact is that money is a necessary part of daily existence.

It's a mistake to become so "spiritual" that you're unable to function effectively in the real world. A spirituality that is divorced from the social and economic realities of our age doesn't serve anyone. If the truth can't flourish in the marketplace, where we all do business with each other every day, what good is it? To be in balance around money is one of the signs that you've integrated your spirituality into your daily life.

If you believe, for example, that money *is* unspiritual, and if you can truly let go of your own need for money and just live a happy and spiritually rich life, then fine—do it. More power to you. But most people who hold this belief struggle with money. Indeed, it is the belief itself, the tendency to cling to one value (spirituality) while resisting the perceived opposite (money) that is behind the struggle. It creates division and conflict.

I began to resolve the money/spirituality split for myself once I realized that true spirituality is not just about personal enlightenment; it manifests itself in a drive to really be there for others, to serve them in a way that helps them draw closer to their spirituality.

Worrying about how to pay the rent and other bills made it hard to focus on being of service to others. Getting money in balance in my own life, I realized—getting *enough* money for my own needs—was essential if ever I was to be of any help to others. As long as I was still worrying about money, I wasn't of much use to anybody.

Money is energy quantified. It's an arbitrary value used to decide how much a particular source, or flow, of energy is worth. The source may be labor or time, goods or services, or an entity or vehicle, such as a business or corporation. The decision as to how much the energy is worth is an agreement between the buyer and seller. The value is negotiated according to the principle of supply and demand—how much of a product or service is available, and how badly someone wants it. This is basic economics.

If you don't decide how much your energy is worth, someone else—with more money smarts than you—will make the decision for you. How you value your time and services monetarily has a lot to do with how you value yourself. If you have a low opinion of yourself, you'll undersell your services. If you have an inflated opinion of yourself, you'll overprice them. Somewhere in the middle there's a healthy balance—the true and actual worth, based on current market conditions, of what is being exchanged.

When you live in balance, you charge a fee that is fair and reasonable. This leaves everybody happy. Or, to say it a little differently: when truth becomes more important than profit, we'll have a world that works.

Money is called "currency" for a reason. The root meaning of the word *current* is "to run," or "to flow." Just as blood circulating in the body carries vital oxygen and nutrients to the cells, so the circulation of money moves or carries into your life the things you need for your survival and well-being. Money is the lifeblood of the material world. It is the material *chi* of the universe. If you're not tapped into a money flow somehow, you have limited access to the things only money can buy.

To generate a money flow, then, you have to put energy out to draw money in. This means that unless you're financially independent, or are on welfare, you need to work—to sell or barter your labor, goods, or expertise—in exchange for money.

When you focus on the quality of the work you're offering, you ensure the optimal return for your efforts. When you focus on the money you expect, your work suffers, people see through you, and you experience diminishing returns.

That's why it's important to get the money issues and agreements handled *before* you begin the job. It frees you up to focus on doing the best work possible. All people who operate with skill and confidence in the world of money do it this way. They are not afraid to talk about money. If you still feel uncomfortable talking about money, or asking for it, then the Money Beliefs process, which I'll describe shortly, will help.

## MONEY AND HAPPINESS

Some years ago I was driving in my car listening to an interview with the late Steve Ross, former CEO of Time Warner, on public radio. It was one of the most frank and personal conversations I had ever heard with such a powerful, high-ranking figure in the corporate world.

He had been diagnosed with terminal cancer. The remarkable thing was his honesty. His exact words are lost in memory, but this is the gist of what I heard this intelligent, learned, enormously successful, and—as I was to discover—surprisingly sensitive human being say.

"I gave my whole life to business, to making deals, building an empire, and amassing a fortune. And I succeeded, obviously, at the highest level. Through it all, however, I never gave any time to self-reflection. I never gave any time to finding out who I was beneath my corporate identity. I never gave any time to the inner, spiritual journey, to discovering the riches that I suspect lie deep within my heart and soul, that lie hidden beneath the outer fabric of life, the surface stuff that consumes so much of our attention."

During the course of the interview he acknowledged that he had exercised a certain ruthlessness to get where he had wanted to go, and that it had negatively impacted his relationships.

Then he added something, with a sincerity so poignant,

that it actually moved me to tears. It was almost as if he was asking God for forgiveness for having been so single-mindedly focused on his own material success.

"And I regret that now," he said. "I regret it deeply. I just hope this disease leaves me enough time to undergo this inner journey, this journey back to my self, my real Self—whatever that is—that I should have started long ago."

I don't know what the final outcome of Steve Ross's inner journey was, but his candor during that radio interview helped bring something home to me. If ever I had any doubt before, it showed me that money and success not only do *not* have anything to do with real inner peace and happiness, but can, in fact—as I suggested earlier—be a barrier to it.

Money gets out of balance when people try to create a far bigger flow of it than they actually need. Then it unbalances them. It takes them out of their heart, away from their essence. They become disconnected from the joy, openness, and spontaneity that is their true nature.

People who get caught in the money trap become so obsessed with financial security that their hearts literally close down. They cease being generous. Money and "things" become more important than human relationships. They may accumulate plenty of material assets, but not without a price. Greed may bring a person a lot of money, but it costs them their soul, their happiness.

Money can buy you pleasure, freedom of time, and a feeling of security. It can even buy you a sense of "happiness," but not the happiness that is without cause. Lose your money—or even think about losing it—and your happiness flies out the window.

Finding balance around money is a matter of knowing your realistic needs and desires and doing just what it takes to satisfy them. If everybody did this, the world would be in balance with money, and everybody would have enough. Greed is what upsets the balance and creates the gap between the very rich and the very poor. Don't let need mushroom into greed. To find out where the balance point is, let go of your ego and look into your heart.

Money *is* important, and it always feels good to make it, to earn it, and to know that you have enough for your needs. If you have *more* than enough, then you're doubly blessed. But let the emphasis on money be secondary to your relationships, your work, your creativity. Just as you must let your ego become the servant of your heart if you want to be happy, so let money be the by-product of the service you render to others.

The process that follows will help clarify the beliefs you presently hold about money. Exploring these beliefs, both the downside and the upside, will give you a more realistic appreciation for just what money can and cannot do. If money is genuinely easy to come by for you, and you have no financial problems or hang-ups, feel free to skip this exercise!

## TOOL #16
### MONEY BELIEFS

At the top of a sheet of paper, or on your word processor, write the statement "The negative/limiting beliefs I have about money." Then, down one side of the paper, begin writing everything that comes up for you in response to that statement. Write as many responses as you can. Aim to get at least a dozen, and as many as twenty. Examples might be:

1. "Money always seems so difficult to come by."

2. "I can't be spiritual and have money."

3. "Other people seem to have a lot more money than I do."

4. "How can I justify having more money when so many have so little?"

5. "I've got so much debt, it seems like I'll never get ahead financially."

6. "If I charge what I feel my service is really worth, people will think I'm greedy."

Then do the Balancing Perceptions process. Take each response, and look at how this belief you have might actually serve you. What's the positive teaching, the gift in it? How might it actually be a blessing in disguise? Examples of this process regarding the above six responses might be:

1. "Maybe I need to relax around money more, to stop grasping and worrying. I need to create more of an abundance consciousness within, so money can flow more easily toward me."

2. "How does this belief square with the fact that I know people who are very successful financially, and yet who are caring, compassionate, and very giving people, too? Maybe if I was truly spiritual, and brought those spiritual values of kindness and loving service into my work, I'd actually make even more money. Then I'd have more money to give away, to help people with."

3. "I can learn from the people who have more money than I do. How do they do it? This is also an opportunity for me to stop comparing, to stop fixating on what others do or don't have, and start connecting with what is true in me."

4. "If I were to become financially independent it would free me up to help others. If I had a lot of money, I could actually use the surplus to do some good."

5. "Debt is a sign that money is out of balance in my life. Again, I need to get more control over my finances. That's the first step to getting ahead. Secondly, a lot of successful business-men carry major debt. Do I need to let debt weigh me down? What if I died in debt? If I was truly free inside, at peace with myself, would it matter? Debt is an opportunity not to take debt—and other money problems—personally."

6. "By my charging what my time and services are really worth, people will value what I do that much more. They are more likely to follow through on my recommendations, because they have an investment in it."

When you've completed the exercise, sit with your responses for a few minutes, then let everything inside your head go. Breathe, center yourself, and relax into the quiet stillness of your own energy. Let your heart open, and sit with this thought: now that you've bal-anced the positives and the negatives, consider the fact that money is just money, a needed means of exchanging energy and value. The beliefs you hold about it, especially the negative ones, simply get in the way of your having an easy, harmonious relationship with money.

Whenever a problematic situation or limiting belief around money arises in the future, quickly counter it by probing for the pos-itive. What's the blessing here? What does this problem have to teach you? How does what you believe about it actually serve you?

---

In some ways, it is the themes presented in this money chapter that formed, when I first began thinking about them, the whole impetus for this book. When I was being over-whelmed with financial challenges, my friend Larry pointed out to me, "Jim, you've been way out of balance around money." Whenever Larry talked about balance, I used to have a lot of resistance to what he was saying. (Funny how we come around, in the end.) To me, the word smacked of compromise—and enlightenment, as far as I was concerned, would admit no compromise. As long as you were trying to balance the spiritual with the material, you could never get really free, I felt. It smacked too much of duality, a trick of the ego. At best, you'd have a little inner peace, while still getting to cling nervously to your stash. How free was that?

When I asked my spiritual teachers about enlightenment and how to deal with the world of money, they would all respond in much the same way: "Do what you have to do, or must do, or want to do to earn a living, but don't get too caught up in that game. Save your main thrust of time and energy for realizing enlightenment. Once you discover the profound ease of being that is your true nature, you'll look out at the world through very different eyes. You'll understand that, whether you have money or not, no real harm can ever befall you."

They were saying, in other words, go for truth above all, but don't neglect your monetary needs and responsibilities. I trusted them, although I often had doubts, too. There was a time, a few years ago, when I seriously began to wonder whether I'd backed the wrong horse. I was having major money problems. I began to think that maybe I'd made a mistake giving so much of my life and energy to the pursuit of enlightenment, and that I should have just, like so many men I knew, gone for the money, for financial success, for material security.

I actually sat with that question in meditation one morning, and ended up giving myself a good talking-to. I reminded myself of the commitment I'd made to fully realize the clarity and freedom that had been revealed to me in one life-changing moment of awakening almost twenty years earlier.

Two years after the health crisis that jump-started my spiritual journey, I woke up one summer's morning, and everything in my mind spontaneously fell away. I lay there, in bed, in the most profound state of clarity, stillness, and oneness I'd ever known. In those few precious moments I perceived the fundamental beauty and perfection of life, and realized that there was nothing to seek.

It, God, the universe, was all right here, and always had been. *It* was my true nature, our true nature. A hole had been punctured permanently in the veil of illusion that was my ego, the "story" of life, and from that morning forward there was no doubt about why I was here: it was to learn how to be in that clear, luminous state of consciousness, of ease, all the time.

Reminding myself of that event during that particular morning meditation was enough to set me straight again. I remembered who I was, and what I stood for. After that, I had no more doubts about the wisdom of the path I'd taken. I knew I was on the right track for me, and that money, while important, could not be the primary focus of my life.

## HARD TIMES

As I said earlier, if you're not tapped into a money flow somehow, you can't move much stuff into your life. Poverty is being out of the flow altogether. "Poverty Sucks" could well be the bumper sticker of our materialistic, consumerist age, but the truth is that poverty only sucks when it's not a choice.

When you consciously choose poverty, or at least a marginal income and lifestyle, then it's not a problem. Nothing is a problem when you choose it. Poverty is only a problem when you feel like a victim of it, when you constantly struggle with and complain about the circumstances you find yourself in.

Why, you might ask, would you "choose" poverty? It's obvious. If you're an artist, writer, or musician, or if you are on a serious spiritual quest, or focusing on your education in some other way, you may well choose to put money-making aside for the time being.

After all, you're pursuing a goal that is much more meaningful to you—the fulfillment of a burning inner quest, a profound creative urge. You're willing to pay whatever price is necessary to achieve your heart's desire. You refuse to be discouraged by either poverty or rejection. You persist, you stay the course, long after most have given up. This, more often than not, is the price of success. It's about taking a stand, and hanging in there.

The money either will or will not come later, depending on how much you really want it. In any case, if you have the soul of an artist or a seeker, you know, intuitively, that your basic needs will always be met.

In a caring society, welfare is needed for those who are incapable of doing work or who are genuinely unable to find it. The problem with living too long on welfare is that it can eventually destroy any initiative to go out and find work. Energy and creativity start to wither. It's almost a law of human nature that if you keep giving someone money, they have little incentive to go out and earn any of their own. While a generous heart is essential for success, sometimes the most loving thing you can do is say no when someone asks you for money.

There are many successful people who will tell you that their own prosperity began when a friend refused to bail them out financially and they realized they had to get out of the hole on their own. The simple and profound truth is that you *can* do it on your own, if you have the intention, the will, the discipline, the vehicle—and the heart.

Dire financial stress is not such a bad thing if it causes you to reevaluate who you are and the way you're living your life. Sometimes, bankruptcy is the only way out. Bankruptcy itself can be a path to enlightenment, if it causes you to give up your attachment to not just your credit rating, but to your self-image, your ego, as well.

I know of quite a few people who have gone through the process and come out the other side wiser, more responsible, and considerably more humble. I went through it myself when my own post-divorce financial problems got completely out of hand. I definitely grew from the experience. Like getting my heart broken, it resulted in a number of unexpected gifts and blessings: I learned to manage my money better, I learned not to make financial agreements that I wasn't able to keep, and I learned—above all—that I wasn't my self-image, my story, and I *wasn't* the conditions of my life.

As you get the core insight and wake up to the truth of your being, you come to the realization that extreme debt and related money problems are, in a way, a form of financial cancer. Just as you would not let even a serious health problem distract you from what you know to be real in life, so you learn not to let financial stress do that, either.

Material conditions are always subject to change, and fortunes—in health, relationships, and finances—rise and fall. The more connected you are to your spiritual nature, to the underlying beauty, and sacredness of life, the more you are fed and sustained by an inner energy, a richness within.

This energy soothes and eliminates any residual patterns of fear that may arise. You are able to see your situation with clarity and compassion. Then you can take appropriate action, and accept whatever learning is there to be had.

### CREATING MORE OF A FLOW

One of the most important steps in turning hard times around is to stop talking about your money problems, to stop telling people how difficult things are for you. Trust me, this *really* works. It cannot be emphasized enough: when you talk about your problems, whether to yourself or others, you just perpetuate them.

I was going to the bank one day to deposit a sizeable insurance check that had come in—a payment due me that I'd forgotten about. I was reflecting on the fact that when I needed money, it always seemed to show up in my life—and that the limiting beliefs I held around money, and the way I talked to my friends about it, were actually inconsistent with the truth of my experience. In my consciousness, I still had this idea that, for me, money was always a problem, and there was never going to be quite enough of it.

From that day forth, I resolved to stop talking about my money difficulties. Indeed, I made a pact with myself to stop *thinking* about money in a negative way. I gave myself a new mantra, an affirmation: "Money keeps showing up in my life. I have plenty of money."

Since that day, there has always been enough money, and I have felt inwardly wealthy and trusting in a way I never did before. Interestingly, about eight months after that revelation, I went through a period when, for a few weeks, finances got really tight again—as they can well do, from time to time.

The first thing I said to myself was, "Well, Jim, you were getting used to having money again. You were starting to get a little *attached*." In other words, I was starting to take money for granted once again—a dangerous state of mind indeed. Learn from the wealthy. They *never* take their wealth for granted, especially if they've worked hard to earn it.

I immediately did two things. I worked on releasing the inner attachment to the outer material state of my life (that is, I reminded myself that I was not my financial circumstances), and I got to work on generating revenue. Specifically, I made phone calls to collect some money that was owed me. Within a few days my financial ship was cruising steadily again. (I call this two-phase process for restoring balance Remembering, and it's one of the powerful tools I'll share with you in the last chapter.)

Jesus gave to us what is probably the most profound teaching on abundance that has ever been revealed: "To him who has, it shall be given, and he shall have more abundance; but whoever has not, it shall be taken away."

Does this sound a little bit like saying the rich get richer, and the poor get poorer? Sound a little unfair? You may well wonder why Jesus would make such a statement. He surely didn't want the rich to get richer, and the poor to get poorer, did he?

We must remember, though, that Jesus taught in parables, in metaphors. It's true that money attracts money. When you already have a lot of money it's easier to borrow more, your investments earn high yields (your money makes money for you whether you are sleeping, playing, or watching television), you can hire lawyers and accountants to find you more tax breaks, and people want to do business with already successful people.

By the same token, people who feel like they are always going to be broke will *stay* broke, simply because they have crystallized around a belief system—and if they were to start making money, it would go against their belief system. Having been there myself, I have empathy for the "financially challenged," but I also have more insight now into how the process of manifestation works. You have to develop the *consciousness* of life's fundamental goodness and abundance, first, and then the outer supply—the money itself, or whatever—can come to you.

If you want to bring more money into your life, you must *release* all the limiting beliefs, such as "I'm broke," "I'll never get ahead," etc. Even though generating more money may seem hopeless or unlikely at this moment, in order for it to happen you must first create a receptivity in your own consciousness. If you stay fearful and contracted, you're blocking the infinite potential that is out there from coming your way. And it *is* out there. It's not as if there's a shortage of money—or of anything else—in this world of ours.

This is what Jesus was referring to. He was speaking of an inner richness, a richness of spirit. If you want to manifest more money in your life, you must first generate the consciousness of more money. You must feel yourself to be rich and full inside— and this is where the spiritual work comes in. (It is also why mere positive thinking alone usually isn't enough. You can't do it in your mind, through tinkering around with thoughts and concepts. You must feel it in your *heart,* in your soul, in the depths of your being.)

So, it is through your inner, spiritual work that you tap into the fullness and richness of your true nature—the treasure, the kingdom, within. Then you move out into the world, into the marketplace of your work or your business, with that consciousness. And what a difference it makes, when you do business from a place of inner joy, of an expectancy *without* attachment. Watch the business that begins to flow your way!

The following tool was given to me by Larry, my mentor in the material realm. It provides specific practical steps for generating the revenue you need. The 10% savings step is something I've added into the process.

### TOOL #17
### MANIFESTING THE MONEY YOU NEED

This is a simple exercise, one that you can do each month. You get very clear about the bills and payments you have due, the money you need to bring in to cover them, and then any extra you'd like for investment, vacation, special purchases, and the like. Be realistic in the figures you settle on. Balance optimism and hope with current economic reality. Once you see how this works, you can begin to push the envelope as you reach for higher financial goals. Now take a sheet of paper, then write down the following:

1. *How much* money you need.

2. *What* you need it for (the itemized list of individual bills, expenses, etc.).

3. *When* you need it by.

Then put the sheet of paper in your checkbook. You've set your intention, and now you can let it go. Focus on the work before you. You'll be surprised by what happens.

Second, each time you make a deposit into your checking account, write out a check to yourself for 10% of the amount and put it into a special savings account. If you're making your deposit at the ATM, you can deduct and transfer the 10% right there, as part of the same transaction.

You may find it a good idea to have several savings accounts, each of them earmarked for a special purpose, such as "Vacations," "Home Purchase Fund," etc. If you're self-employed, you can also have a "Taxes" savings account, so that each time you make a deposit, you put a portion aside—15% of your gross, of whatever the figure is—for taxes. That way, you won't get stuck at the end of the quarter, or the end of the year.

---

There's enough money circulating out there. You just have to learn how to tap into the current. You do this by creating a vehicle to bring money into your life—a job, a business, a service, a product (or something else you can sell), or an investment portfolio. As your understanding about money grows, creating a sufficiency of it will become easier.

The "trick," the one that has to be learned over and over again, is to keep your ego out of your handling of money. In a society that values money more than just about anything else this isn't easy to do. Keep your heart continually open, learn to love truth more than money, and you won't be seduced by society's agenda.

Eventually you'll arrive at the state of consciousness where you *know* the money is going to come. You just know that the money will always be there when you need it. The interesting part is waiting to see *how* it will come—and the unexpected places it comes from!

If you're not connected to your spiritual source, if you don't have a deep and abiding sense of your own innate worth as a human being, you'll always be insecure and anxious around money. Finding balance in the world of money, work, relationships, and everything else begins to happen effortlessly as you awaken spiritually, as you tap into the freedom that is your true nature.

As one of my teachers, Dr. R. P. Kaushik, said, enlightenment doesn't guarantee you'll be able to pay the rent. But (as I've learned), it *will* enable you to stay relaxed and at peace while you go about your business, generating whatever energy might be needed to facilitate the money coming in.

To feel love in your heart, and depth and richness in your soul—this is the true abundance and prosperity. Give this energy to the world, share it with others, and people will be happy to pay you for your services. Find a way to create *value* for other people, and value will come back to you. Ask anyone you admire who has both a good heart and is successful in the world, and they will attest to the truth of this. Be generous in paying others, whether with your energy or your money, and your generosity will come back to you tenfold.

Sometimes people have to lose all their money before they get the lesson around unconditional giving, the importance of not being attached to money. Remember that money is only a *measure* of energy. What is really being exchanged is energy. When you're generous with your energy, you open a constant flow of energy in your life. It comes from the source, flows through you, goes out to others, and returns.

Open your heart, be generous, and you'll always be in the flow.

## ACCUMULATION AND BALANCE

Non-attachment doesn't mean not being responsible. To keep things in balance, you must exert a gentle but firm control over the flow of money in your life.

To practice getting better control over your money, try the image of a reservoir and a valve. The reservoir is your "pool" of money. Keep the "in" valve open so there's nothing to stop money from entering your pool. Welcome all that comes. When someone wants to give you money, accept it gladly—unless you really *don't* need it.

When you need to pay money out, be careful about how far you open the "out" valve. Prioritize your bills and obligations. Judiciously direct the outward flow of money to exactly where it's needed, and nowhere else.

If you leave the "out" valve so wide open that your money pours out without your even noticing where it's going, your pool will soon run dry. This is what makes people broke. Some of us, then, need to learn to exert a tighter grip over our money, to hold on to it more. Others of us, who have problems with generosity, need to learn to let go. Do whatever is necessary to find the balance.

The way to never have any money is to spend too much, or spend unwisely. The first step in accumulating money is to get control of your income and expenses. As money begins to accumulate in your life, your pool will grow. Eventually there will be a surplus, which you'll be able to invest. Then you can watch the interest on your investments grow. One day, if you're fortunate, the interest alone may meet all or most of your obligations. You won't have to touch your pool, your capital.

When you live off your capital, your financial "corpus," you can be absolutely sure of one thing—your pool will eventually dry up. The rich understand this. They are called "capitalists" because they have mastered the art of preserving, of holding on to, their capital. The rich never touch their capital, and thus they grow richer.

One of the reasons why the rich have more money is that they manage it better. They understand the rules of the money game. There are two important lessons you can learn from observing them. The first is patience. Rich people are usually very patient. They are willing to wait. They don't indulge every momentary spending whim or urge. They have the long view. They know that accumulation is a function of planning, time, and steadfastness. They work patiently toward their financial goals.

The second lesson has to do with the price the rich often pay for their wealth. Remember, you don't get something for nothing in this world. Because their gaze is frequently somewhere in the future, on continued accumulation and preservation of their assets, the rich tend to miss the moment. They miss the joy that comes from simply *being.*

The rich also tend to worry a lot about losing their money.

Attachment, remember, breeds fear. It's hard to relax and enjoy the beauty of the moment if you're always worrying about how your net worth is doing. It's hard to be open and spontaneous if you've spent most of your life trying to control the outcome of every transaction, every deal, every relationship.

This fear is behind the lack of generosity exhibited by a lot of people who have money. They are tightwads. Their hearts are closed down. They could give more to others and help out a lot without hurting themselves, but they don't.

The enlightened rich find a way to share their excess wealth. This is the meaning of philanthropy—a love of mankind. The sooner the rich get enlightened, the sooner we'll see some real changes in the distribution of wealth in the world.

When it comes to money, the balance—as always—is to be found in the middle. Managing your resources well, controlling your expenses, accumulating enough assets to take care of you and your family, is a smart move.

When you get money in balance in your life, you free yourself from the anxiety and preoccupation that plague you when it's out of balance. You free up your energy for helping others and enjoying your life. Understand how money works, how it flows and circulates, and your relationship with money—getting it, keeping it, using it—will become easier.

When your relationship with money starts to become more of an effortless process for you, then you're in true alignment with the universe. This alignment happens naturally as you learn to put integrity before money. Never dilute the truth for the sake of money or popularity. Don't sell out.

Balance is a beautiful dance, but when things get out of balance, it can lead to disaster. The key to finding balance around money is in the heart. Handle your financial affairs with a clear mind and a loving heart, and money won't be a problem for you.

The final tool in this chapter will do one of two things. If you don't have enough money, it will help generate the inner consciousness that will attract more money to you. Conversely, if you have plenty of money but still feel that there's something missing in your life (such as inner peace, happiness, or love), this will help you open your heart so you can access more of those inner qualities that money can't buy.

## TOOL #18
## THE GATES OF GENEROSITY

Sit, meditate, get centered. Breathe, feel yourself in your body. Let your awareness expand to embrace your body, the objects in the room, the sounds you hear. Let your awareness become one with the space around you, and the spaciousness you feel inside your body. Then, as you center your awareness in your heart, right in the middle of your chest, begin to reflect on the flow of money in your life.

Is the flow working or not? Is money in balance in your life? Could you be managing it better, or more conscientiously? Do you need to clarify your financial goals? Do you need to explore other ways of generating revenue?

How generous are you—not just with money, but with your time, your attention, your love? Is there any person or situation you are withholding yourself from in some way? Could you give more of yourself to them? Can you be more present? Can you be more liberal with your praise?

As you breathe down into your belly, let your chest expand and your heart fill. Open your eyes. Gaze out at the room, the view out the window. Feel your connection to the physical environment around you, to life itself. Feel the love that life, God, creation has for you. It's brought you safely to this point, hasn't it? Maybe things aren't so great in your life right now. Maybe there are health, relationship, or financial problems. But you're still here, still alive, still in the game. You still have another chance to get tuned in, to be fully conscious and awake. Be thankful for that.

Then meditate on these words: "Gratitude opens the gates of the heart, and the key to abundance is a generous, loving heart. As I learn to trust and open my heart more of everything I long for will flow into my life. This includes inner peace, happiness, love, and money."

---

## THE SPIRITUAL ECONOMY

In his book *The Celestine Prophecy,* James Redfield weaves into an adventure story nine insights about the transformation of humanity. The ninth insight refers, in part, to a planetary economy based on trading money for spiritual wisdom. As people value spiritual insight more, they will be willing to pay those who bring it to them. Redfield envisions that such spiritual "transactions" will eventually replace the current market economy and the need for paid employment.

It is a radical idea, and one that goes against the grain of traditional spiritual teachings, where the teachings are usually given free, or at least kept as far removed as possible from the taint of money. Consider, for example, these words from Kabir Helminski, an American Sufi leader, interviewed in *Yoga International* magazine: "There can be no profit motive in sharing the knowledge of illumination; if there is, both sides are being poisoned. A professional class of spiritual advisers does not fit with the truth and eventually corrupts it. Sufi teachers have always been required to earn a livelihood apart from spiritual teaching and never to receive payment for spiritual guidance. In Islam, knowledge isn't for sale."

What to make of these two seemingly contradictory views?

I think both are right, and in the new millennium I believe we will see more of an integration of the two perspectives. Redfield's idea makes sense in that, as more and more people seek out the liberating truth of enlightenment, they will need the time and teachings of those who are able to bring it to them. They will be more than willing to pay money (as they are already doing) for books, audio and video tapes, and for lectures, seminars, workshops, and retreats.

The teachers, in turn, need to earn a living just like anyone else. Many of them have families to support and children to educate. Unless they are financially independent, are being supported by a patron or benefactor, or have some other means, they will need to receive payment of some kind for the work they do, whether on a donation basis or as an actual fee.

The true teacher knows that the "knowledge of illumination" is, indeed, priceless, and will always freely share his or her wisdom with anyone who seeks it. However, the knowledge itself is frequently packaged with a variety of techniques and practices that address specific personal or worldly problems and issues, and make it easier to understand and embody the teaching. These practices, which may include yoga, bodywork, healing, psychotherapy, awareness training, energy work, counseling, and coaching, derive from the teacher's special or professional expertise, and it is usual and customary to charge for them.

How much to charge will depend upon a number of variables, including the time involved and the administrative and logistical expenses associated with making the teaching available. If the client or student cannot afford the fee but really wants the work, a compassionate teacher will always find a way of delivering it, either through a payment plan, work exchange, scholarship, or gift.

The point to remember, if you are a teacher and are grappling with the money issue, is that the ultimate goal is enlightenment, or transformation, of the student. Money may well be involved in the transaction at some point, but it must be handled cleanly , it must be secondary to the student-teacher relationship, and it must never be a barrier to the delivery of the teaching.

I don't, however, believe the "spiritual economy" will replace the market economy—precisely because I don't differentiate between the two. You can't really draw a line between the spiritual and material. We may use these terms to differentiate between the inner and outer aspects of life, but there is actually only one reality, consciousness, manifesting in an infinite diversity of forms.

We need the means of exchanging goods and services—the "market" economy. But as humanity's consciousness continues to evolve and transform, people will transact business more from their hearts, and less from their heads; of that I have no doubt.

As people throughout the world begin to wake up spiritually and learn to value others for both who they are *and* their willingness to contribute, to take care of themselves and be financially responsible, we will see a gradual, worldwide social, cultural, and economic transformation. Of this I am also sure.

More and more of us in the developed countries will start tapping into the fullness of being that is our true nature. We won't need or want to consume as much materially, because of our inner spiritual abundance. We won't need all the distractions, diversions, and enticements that fuel so much of the market economy, and most of Madison Avenue's advertising. We'll buy a lot less, and be much more discriminating in what we buy.

Our current economy is built upon the mass of consumers feeling empty, feeling that something is missing from their lives and that they *need* this new soap, perfume, bedroom set, suit of clothes, computer, or car to keep them competitive and make them happy. The need for consumption drives production. The sources of production, in turn, have a vested interested in reinforcing, in the minds of consumers, the illusion of need, hunger, and emptiness.

When the need for consumption diminishes, not just because of an economic recession but also because people are becoming enlightened and their buying habits are changing, what will that do to the economy? How will things look in the twenty-first century? I submit that nobody can actually know yet, because it will be an organic process, appropriate to the exact needs of the time. It will be a whole new economic paradigm, one that will unfold and take shape as *we* unfold within, and apply our wisdom and creativity to balancing our inner and outer needs.

It will certainly involve a fairer and more equitable distribution of the immense wealth that now exists in the world, but it won't be Communism. That was tried for more than fifty years, and it didn't work. You can't force people to give up their freedom, or deny their individuality or creativity. Besides, Communism's fundamental error was that it lacked a spiritual dimension. The whole Marxist edifice was built upon the belief in the power of man, and man alone isn't enough.

But it won't be pure capitalism, either. Capitalism is Darwinism applied to economics, where only the strong prevail while the economically weak, who in theory have the same opportunities as the rich, in practice get squeezed out of the money-making game.

The downfall of capitalism is that it too readily permits wealth and power to be concentrated in the hands of the few. It makes man God, and denies the true God—the interconnectedness of *all* of life. By holding out the promise that others can have the same opportunities while preventing them from doing so through the practice of monopolization, the all-powerful gods of capitalism get to keep the rest of us off their backs while they play their exclusive—and often heartless—game.

The new economy, the true "spiritual" economy, won't follow any particular rules or dogmas other than the fundamental economic principle of supply and demand. When the law of supply and demand is balanced by and mediated through commonsense values and a loving, compassionate heart, then everything always works out financially. Many conscious individuals are already demonstrating this truth in their private financial lives. They are finding a balance between productivity and leisure, between satisfying wants and needs, between voluntary simplicity and measured affluence, between steady accumulation and generous giving.

To understand this way of living, to see the beauty and potential in it—and, above all, to come to the place where you *trust* the creative process, the divine goodness of life—you have to first come to real freedom within yourself. You have to find the source of love and happiness within yourself, independent of the outer conditions in your life. You have to understand, embody, and live the core insight that is the key to the way of harmony. The next—and final—chapter will remind you of just what it takes to do this.

CHAPTER SEVEN

# Maintaining the Balance

## BECOMING FEARLESS

*T*here are three levels of enlightenment. (Dance lightly with this, now! This is just one way of looking at it.)

The first is self-acceptance, coming to terms with who you are at a human, personal level—faults, flaws, and all. It's enlightenment at the psychological and emotional level. You're not fully at peace yet, and you still have fears and concerns, but they don't control you anymore.

The second is opening to the presence of the divine. It's tuning in to and sensing the underlying unity, beauty, and sacredness of life. This is being awake to spirit. You're still fairly attached to the idea of "you" as the person who experiences spirit, who practices awareness, or mindfulness. But you're really starting to open up to a dimension beyond your own, limited self. You can access, at will, the inner dimension, the ground of harmonious being. It's no longer just a random event for you. The personal sense of fear is beginning to leave you, and peace is becoming more real.

Most people go back and forth between the first and second

levels, and you must be established in both before you can successfully break through to the third.

The third level is self-realization, true inner freedom. It is awakening to the realization that you *are* the divine, that you are an instrument of God, or whatever you want to call the intelligence and power behind creation. You no longer perceive or experience yourself as separate from this power. You still have your unique individuality, or personhood, but at a fundamental level you know that you and it are one. You are *That,* as the Upanishads say.

At the first level, you're starting to feel good about who you are. At the second, you're starting to connect with the energy, the power, that made you who you are. At the third level, you no longer think about who or what you are. You're just *being* who you are.

The core insight brings you to the third level. It frees you from your story, from the illusion of self, the fixed idea of "I am this," or "I am that." You no longer need to hold on to any psychological or emotional definition of self, and this brings a feeling of real confidence, of divine fearlessness. You know that no harm can befall who you really are. Inner peace is now your abiding reality.

With the letting go of the attachment to self, the mind is flooded with light (hence the term "en-*light*-enment"), just as when you release a tight muscle, new energy stirs in your body. When you live free of the idea of being "somebody," you discover who you *really* are—and, with it, a joy that is continually self-renewing.

Of course, you're still *somebody*. You're still a person. You're still *you*. You're just not attached to any *concept* of you. If somebody then asks who you are, you'll respond with whatever is appropriate in the moment (at the third level of enlightenment, living becomes truly spontaneous), but you won't make a big deal out of it.

You'll shift the conversation away from yourself. You just won't be all that interested in talking about yourself. As far as you are concerned, who you are and what others think of you isn't important.

People who are still looking for themselves, however—who are still seeking happiness and fulfillment—usually talk about themselves a lot. They are pretty self-obsessed. This is natural. You're going to be quite concerned with yourself—until you no longer are!

To let go is to detach. Detachment isn't easy at first because you're detaching from your illusions, all the precious beliefs and notions around which you've built your personal identity—and until you know yourself at a spiritual level, your personal identity means everything to you. In fact, it's all you've got. The idea of letting go of it can be very scary. It's no wonder people invest so much energy in defending and justifying their story, in seeking validation and approval for their "self" image.

But detachment gets easier with insight, with deep inquiry into who and what you really are. Eventually, you come to the realization that the self you've been attached to for so many years isn't even real. The concepts, memories, beliefs, and ideas that constitute your internal psychological reality are just appearances in your mind. When you actually see this, the appearances dissolve, and there is just the clear, shining light of awareness, of being. That's freedom!

See the world around you for what it is—a constant whirl of activity and events. When you project your thoughts out into it, when you get attached to or identified with it, you get sucked into the spin. You get pulled off-center. Rein your mind back in. Live in the world, but don't lose yourself in it. Keep to your center.

Let go of your ego, listen to your heart, and you'll be free. You'll be fearless. With awakening, all fear leaves you. But to see through the illusion of fear, you have to first face whatever fears are still controlling you. Here is a tool, an exercise, that can be extraordinarily powerful in helping you do this. I've used it many times to work through the fears that once exerted such a grip on me.

## TOOL #19
## FACING YOUR FEARS

Sit down in meditation. Breathe, relax, get centered. You're going to prepare yourself to take a look at what it is you're currently most afraid of. You sit, steel yourself, and get ready to meet your worst fear. You breathe deeply, stay in your body, and become a spiritual warrior. You face your fear and you work through it.

You play out all the possible scenarios: "What if *this* happened, how would I feel?" "What if *that* happened, how would I feel?" You uncover the different levels of fear, layer by layer. You visualize the worst possible situation—and then you look and see what the actual effect will be, and how you will feel once the thing most feared has come about.

You've got to remember to breathe and to stay very present in your body as you do this. If the feelings get too intense, take a break. Come back to the process later, or the next day. But the idea is to keep doing it over and over again, in as many subsequent meditations as it takes, until you are able to look this once deepest fear of yours squarely in the eyes, and realize that it no longer has any power over you. The thoughts and images that have been holding it together literally begin to break apart. They cannot stand up in the light of your awareness, and your own sense of presence and power just grows stronger.

Let me give you an example, one that I touched on in the last chapter. It's one that many people can relate to. It had to do with a long-held fear I had about survival—a lingering fear that my business would sooner or later dry up, the checks would stop coming in. I'd run out of money, and I'd find myself on the street or having to live under a bridge. Then I'd have to deal with not only the practical struggles of that, but also the shame of wondering what others would think of me. This was a fear I really wanted to be free of, because I knew it was a barrier to the enlightenment I sought.

Facing the fear in meditation, actually seeing, visualizing myself homeless and trying to find refuge under a bridge, with all the misery and deprivation that would imply, brought me to the same realization facing all my other fears did. I may not like living under such circumstances, but I knew that, whatever happened, I would be okay. (Visualizing myself as a Western version of a wandering Zen master somehow made it more palatable.)

I knew who I was at a spiritual level, and I was at peace with myself. I knew that I could handle whatever situation I was confronted with, no matter how awful. I was bigger than whatever conditions or circumstances I was experiencing. I knew how to tune in to the incredibly healing and renewing power of the present, and that that power was always here to sustain, nourish, and guide me.

---

As you face your own fears in this way, you come to understand the truth in that old Irish saying, "If you run away from a ghost, it will chase you and haunt you for the rest of your life, but if you stop, turn, and face it, it will disappear—because ghosts aren't real."

Your fears are not real, either. It's just the thoughts and pictures in your mind that keep them alive. See this, and you'll be free. Then you can move and act in the world with courage, with heart. There won't be anything holding you back from being who you really are.

You will have learned the secret of the samurai warrior, the secret that is the source of his strength and his fearlessness. You will have learned to "die before you die."

## BREAKING THROUGH

What a blessing it is, as you get free of self. As you get free of any need to label or qualify yourself. As you learn to abide, simply, in pure awareness, openness, being. The more you do this, the more you prepare the ground for the breakthrough in consciousness that will really set you free. Let me tell you how it happened for me.

For many years I fluctuated between feeling somewhat contracted and out of balance, and feeling expanded and really in sync with the universe. All my spiritual techniques and practices were focused on doing whatever it took to move from the experience of conflict into a state of ease.

Yet, even as my overall feeling of well-being and confidence improved and became more stable, there was still the feeling that something—the true freedom I sought—was eluding me. I was still stuck at the first and second levels of enlightenment. There was still a "me" holding on to something. I'd still have periods of dissatisfaction, yearning, of something missing. I still hadn't quite "got" it. I went back and forth between feeling spiritually tuned in and on top of things, and feeling like a victim. I was still holding on to an image of myself as a "seeker," as someone who was still looking for something.

Then, a few years ago, during a time when I was going through some particularly challenging personal circumstances, I woke up one spring morning feeling depressed. My normal pattern would have been to get out of bed feeling somewhat low, and then go and sit on my meditation cushion and just breathe, center myself, open to spirit, and wait for the negative energy to clear.

But this morning I lay in bed and faced myself in a way I never quite had before. I was sick of saying "I feel this . . ." or "I feel that . . ." and remaining trapped in some cycle, however minor, of conflict and unfulfillment. I had been listening to my spiritual guide, Jean Klein, say for years that I was not the person I took myself to be. His teaching had taken root in me. Perhaps it was just that I was now ready to face whatever this last vestige of "me" was.

As I lay in bed I got really present, and put the question to myself, "So, *who* is depressed?" and probed deep into the interior of my own consciousness to find this "me" who insisted he felt depressed.

Of course, I couldn't find it. "I" and "me" don't exist, except as concepts, appearances, in the mind. As my awareness opened and expanded, the three thought-forms—"I-feel-depressed"—dissolved, and "I" (as awareness, as consciousness) felt perfectly okay! I got out of bed, sat for a while in meditation, and reflected upon this sense of ease and expansion I now felt, and the process of self-inquiry that had led me to it. Then I went happily about my day.

The same thing happened the next two mornings in a row. I woke, felt depressed, and lay there with the same deep inquiry into "who" was depressed. Each time, the self-concept of "I" or "me" dissolved, the energy in my body and mind reharmonized itself, and "I" felt fine.

In the months following that third morning, it became increasingly evident that I was no longer seeking anything spiritually. I was no longer able to take my personal sense of self seriously. Indeed, whenever I stopped to look inside my own consciousness, I couldn't find that old, solid sense of "me"—the person I'd believed myself to be for the previous forty-plus years—anywhere. It had evaporated like the illusion it always was. In its place there was just a feeling of inner clarity and freedom that was constant and stable, and that nothing seemed to shake.

Occasionally something would happen to cause upset (and, once in a while—inevitably—still does). But then *I*, as awareness, the consciousness that expresses through this body/mind/ego, would quickly remember that I was neither the circumstance nor the story about it, and the sense of being a "somebody" with a problem would dissolve, to be replaced by a feeling of openness, relaxation, well-being.

About a year after that spring morning, I wrote in my journal, "I've found the way Home, now I'm learning to find my way in the world." Once we have seen that we are *not* the "person," the psychological/emotional entity we used to think we were, all seeking falls away (who is there to seek?) and there is no going back. This is the core insight in a nutshell.

Residues of the past, the old ego patterns, arise from time to time—especially during periods of stress or illness—but they are quickly seen through and released. You still have an identity at a personal level, and you still play certain roles in life, but you know now that these are not who you really are. This knowing is accompanied by a profound feeling of inner joy, gratitude, and humility.

What a gift it is to be born as this consciousness, this awareness, manifesting through this particular body/mind!

## EVERYTHING IS POSSIBLE FOR A MIND THAT IS FREE

Psychological thinking is any thinking that emphasizes the pronouns "I," "me," or "mine." It comes out of the past, the personal history you've built up out of all your emotionally charged memories.

Discover for yourself how liberating it is to eliminate excessive use of the words "I," "me," and "mine" from your thoughts and speech. You can actually do this as an experiment.

In fact, I'll offer a challenge to you: once you've put this book down, and the very next time you get into conversation with someone—anyone—direct your attention *away* from yourself. Have a conversation in which you give yourself permission to talk about anything *except* yourself—perhaps by focusing on the other person, and what's happening for them. And, as you talk, be really aware of the words that are coming out of your mouth. Be aware of yourself as the awareness behind the words. Notice how all this feels to you. Notice what you learn. Try it again in other conversations.

Don't deny your past, but don't get hooked into it, either. When memories, images, or emotions surface, simply observe them, witness them. Breathe into the feelings and sensations. Don't hold on to anything. Let everything pass through you.

Even medical science is now confirming the damage done by the ego. An article in *Newsweek* (March 6, 1995) stated: "Studies have found that self-absorption, as manifested by the frequency with which a person uses words like 'I,' 'me,' and 'mine,' makes heart attacks more likely."

To begin getting free of your own story, ask yourself the question Who am I? and then try not to formulate any conceptual answers. If conceptual answers persist in coming, keep letting them go until they all fall away. The important thing is to live with the question. Listen for the deep silence that follows the question. In that silence you'll sense the fragrance of your real being. It will dawn on you one day that your real nature is silent awareness, presence.

Vary the question according to whatever is bothering you at

the time. When you're feeling afraid, ask, "Who is it that's afraid?" When angry, "Who is it that's angry?" When lonely, "Who is it that's alone?"

When you want something badly and are frustrated because you're not getting it, ask: "Who is it that wants?" "Who is it that desires?" or "Who is it that's frustrated?" Or, when you feel depressed, do as I did that spring morning, and ask yourself, "So, who is depressed?"

As with "Who am I?" don't get caught up in intellectual answers. There's no end to them. Go deeper into the silence that follows the question. Find out who you are behind all your ideas about who you are. You'll be blown away by what you discover.

To meditate is to cleanse yourself of the psychological burden of the past. When you need information from your memory banks, it will come to you. But the past won't be a problem.

In freeing yourself from psychological and emotional memory, you have total access to *functional* memory—the accumulated wisdom of a lifetime of learning. Your intuitive powers will also expand. You'll trust your intuition more and more.

You'll no longer worry about the future. As you let go of being constrained, defined, or boxed in by a "personal" history, you'll live more fully in the present moment, and the future itself will be seen in perspective.

Honor the past, keep an eye on the future, but stay firmly grounded in the present—in that place of clarity, poise, and balance. Do this, and you'll have discovered the secret of true happiness.

One of my favorite cartoons shows a yogi in a loincloth sitting on a bed of nails somewhere in a desert. He is surrounded by a hostile environment of cacti and jagged rocks. Another yogi is standing nearby with his hands behind his back, gazing down at him with an inquiring look. The yogi on the bed of nails looks up and says, "It only hurts when I exist."

Pain is a fact of life. Being in a body means you'll always be at risk for pain. Illnesses and injuries happen. But suffering is related to the person, the "I" or "me" who resists and fears the pain. Free yourself from the attachment to "I" and "me," and you'll find that pain, if it comes, is surprisingly bearable.

In fact, the more spaciousness there is inside you, the more likely you are to experience healing at the physical level. It also becomes easier to consciously direct your own healing energy, if needed, in the way that I describe in chapter 1.

When your suffering is particularly intense and you realize it's not going to pass any time soon, just remember: you will get through it. You have to start visualizing yourself getting through it.

A day will come when you'll no longer suffer for yourself, but you'll feel the suffering of others more acutely. You'll feel it because you've been there. This is the awakening of compassion. As you reach out to people in the ways you can, they will feel your calmness, your clarity, your centeredness. Just by being who you are, you'll be a healing presence in their lives.

As they talk about their pain and problems, they may well ask you, "Do you ever get upset? Do you ever lose it? Are you ever gripped by fear, despair, hopelessness?" You'll look them in the eye, and you'll simply tell them the truth—the truth with love.

Yes, you used to get stressed, anxious, and fearful, but one day—as the result of many years of inner work—you woke up to your true nature. With awakening came a wonderful discovery, one of the great lessons of being spiritually free in a human body: shit still happens, you just no longer take it personally!

But you'll also add that, because you're just an ordinary person like anyone else, sometimes you *do* have an initial personal reaction, especially if something really heavy is coming down. The "I" thought arises, the personal self comes into the picture and starts to run its old pattern ("Oh, God, how am *I* going to deal with this?") but then you, as awareness, as consciousness, remember that the "story" is not who you are.

So you let go of the concepts and thoughts, especially the "I" or "me" thought—and you just come back to pure awareness, clarity, presence. And then you deal with the situation. You take whatever action is needed. If it's something really painful, like the loss of someone close to you, of someone you love, you're naturally going to grieve. You're going to feel really sad. You may even be overwhelmed by sadness.

But you don't get lost in personal identification, in "I" or "me." Your *heart* feels the pain, but your ego, your analyzing, judging "I," stays in the background, where it belongs.

Eventually, the grief will run its course (to everything there is a season) and you'll once again find yourself calm and relaxed, breathing in and enjoying the beauty of life in the present.

## WAKING FROM THE DREAM

Dreams change as you open up to your true nature. When you stop identifying yourself with the waking dream, when you stop taking everything so personally, the inner freedom you experience during the day continues through the night.

You still dream at night, but you're no longer identified with the content of your dreams. You're free of being the dreamer. Dreams happen, but there's nobody to whom they're happening. There's a natural detachment, an ease. Just as there is no longer any fear in your consciousness during the day, so there is none at night, which means an end to scary dreams and nightmares.

Dreams are seen for what they are: a direct reflection, a mix-and-match reprocessing, of things you've noticed and experiences you've had during that day. For the most part they are meaningless, just a movie unfolding in your sleeping mind, a way for the unconscious to clear itself of accumulated images and experiences. If you've encountered a lot of negative energy, some of that may leak into your dreams. But, again, you're not identified with it. It's just the deeper levels of your psyche releasing, clearing, and eliminating.

Because you're not personally identified with what's happening in the dreams, you don't seek meaning in them. When you awaken to your true nature, living itself, each unfolding moment, is revealed to be endlessly rich in meaning. Just to *be* is itself immensely meaningful. But the separate self, or ego, is always seeking meaning.

Occasionally your dreams will reveal something prophetic, or insightful, or perhaps the answer to some practical problem. I have periodically had dreams that, through the positive feelings they inspired, validated what I was doing with my life at the time. Or I'd dream about a certain person and be given a different way of seeing them. When I actually did meet them again, I'd see them with new eyes.

Dreamwork, as practiced by certain schools of psychology, such as the Jungian therapists, can be a rich way of accessing deeper levels of the personal self and of one's spirituality. It is a tool for leading one to greater self-acceptance, peace, and happiness—the first and second levels of enlightenment. But it can also be a trap, a snare to reinforce the personal self and seduce it into being attached—even addicted—to dream analysis and meaning.

Learn from your dreams, but realize their limitation. If you want to move beyond the first and second levels of enlightenment into the real freedom of the third, you're going to have to sit with the questions "So, who is dreaming? Who is the dreamer?" until you see that the dreamer, too, is an illusion—just as ephemeral as the dreams themselves.

## LETTING GO OF THE STORY

Many people on the inner path fear that if they release the attachment to their ego and their story, life will somehow become flat and boring. "It's my personality and my hopes, dreams, and attachments that give my life passion and meaning," they say.

When this concern comes up, I usually respond with something like: "The only thing you'll lose is the manic-depressive quality of existence, the fluctuation between excitement and boredom, hope and disappointment, calm and conflict. What you'll experience in its place is a constancy of ease, of peace, of joy, of love, of bliss—with *those* feelings varying in intensity, so that sometimes they will be very strong, and at other times less so. But you'll always feel really *good*—and the funny thing is, you won't even know it."

"What do you mean?" people ask at this point.

One of the signs of freedom is that you no longer think about how you feel. When you're still identified with your ego and your story, you live in constant insecurity, and you're always concerned about how you feel. You're always worrying about whether your life is unfolding in the way you want it to or not.

But when you wake up to the freedom that is your true nature, you no longer think about yourself or your life in that way. Living becomes much more spontaneous. However, if someone happens to ask how you feel, you'll stop, check in, and realize you feel just fine.

One of the ways we remain stuck in our story is through addictions. Addictions are the shadow, the unconscious elements in the psyche, at work. These are the fears and insecurities we haven't yet faced. They cause the ego to dart everywhere, desperately seeking gratification and release from its tension.

Addictions, whether to food, alcohol, drugs, sex, gambling, or television, bring a temporary release, but, in the end, they lead only to further darkness. The main addiction is to the ego itself—to being "somebody."

So long as you persist in living from your ego, you'll remain caught in conflict. You'll always be thinking and worrying about something. Happiness will still be "out there," dependent on some object or event being a particular way, or on some piece of knowledge or understanding to be gained.

The hardest battle you'll ever face is with your own ego. The key to winning the battle is to stop fighting. Accept your ego for what it is. Embrace it as you would a mischievous child. Let it be there—you need an ego for survival—but let it remain in the background.

Remember that this ego, this self you've believed yourself to be, is a fiction. It's a useful fiction at times, but it's still a fiction. Your personal history and the cultural myths you've grown up with are the story of your life and times. The story is a part of your humanity, and needs to be told, to be shared.

Likewise, we need to hear the stories of those who are suffering, or who are being oppressed. Just be sure not to get lost in the story—not somebody else's, and especially not your own. Then you'll be able to hear the other person's story without getting scared or overwhelmed by it. You'll be able to respond to it with clarity, with wisdom, with love. If action is needed on your part, you'll be a much more effective agent for healing and change.

Like a snake shedding its skin, the layers of self gradually drop away. With each shedding, you emerge more and more as the person you really are. All authentic enlightenment traditions point to the transparency of the ego, the "me," as being the key to finding union with the underlying truth and beauty in life. It doesn't matter how you get this realization, or what spiritual path you take, just that you get to it. As someone once said, "Many paths up mountain, top of mountain same for all."

The only barrier to self-realization, as the great Indian sage Ramana Maharshi said, is the belief that we are not realized. Sometimes I will say to a person who is close to breaking through to the third level of enlightenment but still gets sideswiped by doubt, "Look, start believing that you are already enlightened. You are already there. Because you are. It's your true nature. So start to accept it."

But I always add, "However, don't tell anyone for at least a couple of years."

The reason I say this is that it takes time for the awareness of ourselves as the embodiment of pure consciousness, already and always free, to stabilize. When we start telling people we're "there" when we're not yet fully established in our true nature, we open ourselves up to attack, even ridicule—which just throws us back into self-doubt.

Besides, it's another ego trap to go around proclaiming yourself "enlightened." In many ways, it's the ultimate ego game, because it's the one in which the ego has most at stake— its very existence. As long as the ego is pursuing enlightenment, or thinks it's already enlightened, it gets to stay in control. In Zen they call it the "stink of enlightenment." It's where you have a genuine awakening, and then the ego jumps in and claims the experience for itself.

Believe and trust in yourself inwardly, and outwardly just be an ordinary person, doing the work you came here to do. If you really have broken through, you'll know it, and those who are close themselves will sense it. If someone then happens to ask, "Are you enlightened?" you might even say yes, if it seems appropriate (you're not going to lie), but you won't make a big deal out of it.

You'll direct the attention back to the questioner. After all, he or she is still looking, and if the two of you have a rapport, then you'll naturally launch into the enlightenment conversation, and you might just be in a position to give them the specific directions they are seeking.

## REMEMBERING WHAT IS REAL

The realization that there's something missing from life, that there has to be something more or better or different, is what starts most of us on the inner path.

As long as things are going well, however, most people usually have little interest in looking inward. It generally takes some kind of personal crisis or setback to get them to wake up and examine their lives.

An illness, a death, a divorce, a relationship betrayal, the loss of a job, a financial reversal—any of these can shock us into questioning our cherished beliefs and assumptions. If you've ever suffered a major loss, disappointment, or heartbreak, you'll know what I mean.

Suffering becomes an opportunity for transformation if you look for the lesson in it, if it causes you to inquire more deeply into your life and discover what you need to do to become a freer and happier human being. The good news is that once a lesson has been learned, it doesn't need to be repeated. You get to move on to the next lesson.

If there's a fundamental lesson, it's in learning how to bring yourself back to center whenever you get thrown off-balance by some outer crisis or problem. Here's the technique I use if ever I get caught up in some crisis or event, whether real or imagined, and momentarily forget who I am. This *really* works:

## TOOL #20
## REMEMBERING

For this technique to be effective, you must first make a declaration: you must declare your spiritual well-being and happiness to be your primary focus in life. You declare this because you know now, from experience, that without that sense of inner spiritual well-being and wholeness, you cannot function at your highest and best. You can't think as clearly, and you can't act with as much wisdom and compassion. So, you acknowledge that your spiritual well-being is your foremost priority.

Now for the technique: As soon as something happens in your outer environment to disturb your well-being and cause contraction or fear—such as a loss, a disappointment, a challenging problem, or a crisis—you do two things. Both are equally critical, and while it doesn't ultimately matter which one you do first (as long as both are done), as you become more established in your true nature, you'll instinctively tend to do #1 first. Then, out of that renewed sense of clarity, #2 will follow naturally.

1. You inwardly "remember" who you are and what's real by reminding yourself that you are *not* the problem or the fear by saying to yourself, "So, who is worried here? Who is afraid?" You pose the question, you step back with your awareness, you let your awareness expand. You feel the expansion that is your true nature. You tune in to the fullness and beauty of the now moment.

Remind yourself, again, if you have to, that you are *not* the circumstances in your life, and you are not this ego, this "me," who worries, frets, and feels fear. Who you really are is the divine, ever-full, ever-radiant consciousness that expresses through this body/mind that is you. Remember this always!

2. If action is needed, you move as quickly and decisively as you can to address the problem and deal with it in whatever way is most appropriate. You do what needs to be done.

---

As an example of how this actually works in practice, I remember a time when I found myself questioning the worth of a writing project I was working on. An old, almost forgotten feeling of self-doubt and self-judgment rose up in me. Who was I to be writing about enlightenment and balance? I felt my trust in myself and in life begin to waver.

Then I remembered something: "You don't have to be perfect, Jim. You don't have to be 'perfectly' enlightened. Nobody you know is. You know this feeling will pass, so just let it be."

The desire to be perfect comes out of a deep emotional programming, the belief that others couldn't possibly like or accept us as we are because of our flaws and imperfections. It stems from a feeling of low self-esteem, of unworthiness.

Coming to the realization that I didn't have to be perfect was one of the great liberating moments of my life. It is essential for the first level of enlightenment, self-acceptance; it makes you receptive to the second level, which is sensing and feeling the presence of the divine; and it opens the door to the third, to the realization of authentic inner freedom.

In the case of my writing project, I relaxed completely around it, and when I looked at it again, I saw that it was fine as it was. No additional action needed to be taken. The flaring up of self-doubt was just another opportunity to remember my always perfect spiritual nature and not get hung up on my inevitably imperfect human nature.

## DANCING WITH DESIRE

There's nothing wrong with having desires. It's the willful attachment to them that causes frustration and desperateness. To have desires and goals without being emotionally attached to them is a mark of spiritual maturity. It's also the best way to draw the desired object to you.

The process of dancing with desire is helped as you learn to distinguish between your ego's desires—which are endless, and all too often based on illusion and fantasy—and your heart's desires.

Whenever you feel stuck and are not sure what to do, stop and ask yourself, "What do I *really* want?" Question your own motives. Look deep and listen carefully for what is real.

People sometimes get confused about how to distinguish their true inner voice from all the other voices trying to be heard inside them. Here is the way to tell: if your head is filled with a lot of different voices, understand that they are *all* unreal—they are just voices, the different manifestations of your particular story, including all the judgments and criticisms laid on you by others.

Experiment with letting *all* the voices go. Come back to silence. Feel the power of the present. Listen not to your mind, your head, but to your heart. Get totally quiet inside, tuned in to the energy around you, and then listen for the voice that speaks to you out of that inner silence.

To facilitate this process of tuning in, you have to begin by letting go of wanting things to be different than they are. Then you'll find yourself simply *here*, in the present moment. As you learn to breathe through the restlessness, boredom, and tension you inevitably face as you stop running away from yourself, your energies will begin to gather. You'll no longer be dissipating or dividing your energy in pursuit of objects that can never fulfill you.

To stay with your feelings like this without running off to try and assuage them or compensate for them is the essence of meditation. Go deeper in your mediation, and you'll come up against an emptiness inside you. You may be so used to filling up that emptiness from outside that you won't know how to be with it at first. You'll want to revert to your old behavior and run from it. Take a break, if you must, then come back to it. Face yourself anew.

In exploring the emptiness and the pain it inevitably brings up, you'll understand what is meant by the term "dark night of the soul," which was coined by the Spanish mystic St. John of the Cross. Stay with the process, and eventually it will change. You'll probably go through many "dark nights" on your journey of healing and transformation. Welcome them for the doorways to freedom that they are.

Learn to treat the emptiness—and all such difficult states—as a friend. One day, the energy will shift. The emptiness will start to feel more alive, more vibrant. You're beginning to tap into the fullness of Being itself—the very source of happiness.

The choice is yours. You can achieve temporary happiness, mixed in with a lot of frustration, from trying to gratify your ego's desires. Or you can connect with the source of lasting happiness through letting go of your ego, the addiction to "I," "me," and "mine," and listening to your heart.

Understanding and transforming the nature of desire takes time. You've been conditioned—programmed—by society to look outside yourself and desire approval, status, money, and things in order to be happy. It takes time to shift the way you view reality and find the happiness that bubbles up as you release those ego-based desires.

As you learn to honor your desires without being willfully

attached to them, you'll come to the place where, as the American spiritual master Robert Adams put it, "The world no longer has any power over you."

*That's* how the balance is found. When you're no longer attached to being "somebody," the world, with all its problems, conflicts, and temptations doesn't exert the same grip on your psyche. You're not afraid of anything anymore.

You no longer need material security or success to be happy, because you are already happy. You are genuinely at peace within. And this gives you enormous freedom to move, act, and work in the world in a way that is bold, compassionate, and endlessly creative.

Life becomes so much simpler and more joyful. You feel yourself constantly being guided as if by an unseen hand. You feel as if you are being gently carried along by a divine current. Throughout the day, unexpected opportunities and gifts rain down on you. What a blessing, what grace. This is true abundance. This is the way of harmony.

Every so often, you'll have to choose: do you go left, or do you go right? Do you say yes, or do you say no? Ultimately, you realize, it doesn't matter what choice you make because you are already where you've always wanted to be. You're already fulfilled and at peace within.

But if you go left when maybe you should have gone right, or if you say yes when perhaps you ought to have said no, then you'll find yourself on a detour. You may have some difficulties, problems, hassles to deal with. But this is how you learn to choose correctly. This is how you gather life wisdom and experience. But what a gift to understand that, from the ultimate perspective, there *are* no wrong choices.

This last tool, or technique, will help you make better decisions, decisions that draw on both head and heart, reason and intuition. It will teach you to use all your creative capacities in a way that will ensure the best possible outcome of any decision you need to make.

## TOOL #21
## CHOOSING

When you're faced with a difficult choice or decision, use this three-step process, beginning with your rational mind first.

1. Mentally note, or write down if you prefer, what your *options* are. List the main options, alternatives, or choices facing you.

2. Then take note of the *consequences* of each option. For every decision you make, there is always a consequence. The consequence is usually in the form of a *pro* and a *con,* a benefit and a cost. List the pros and cons in a rational manner and get clear about them. Make sure you're also aware of how the consequences affect others. If you're going to make a decision that will have an effect on other people, especially those who may be close to you, you need to be clear about it.

3. Now comes the fun part. You simply ask yourself this: "Which set of consequences am I most willing to live with? Which ones do I feel most drawn to? Which ones resonate most with my heart, my true Self?"

Each of the consequences carries a certain "energy," has a certain "feel." Some of the consequences will be so repellent that they will automatically eliminate themselves. Thus the choices narrow. If you're still in doubt, look again for the one that has the most energy, that attracts you the most, that supports your freedom and well-being at the deepest level. (And, if it is really good for you, it will be right for others, too.)

---

I will give you an example of how this tool works in practice. I was doing a private consultation with a woman who was participating in a meditation workshop I was leading in New Zealand. The woman, Heather, was experiencing tremendous confusion. She had left her husband and a difficult marriage of fifteen years to go and live with Mark, her yoga teacher. Her husband wanted her back, and Mark wanted her to stay with him.

"I'm not sure what to do," she said, with that panicky look people get when they feel their whole life hinges on the decision confronting them, and that it's the end of the world if they make the wrong one. "I don't really want to go back to my painful marriage, and while I really like Mark, and we have great chemistry together, I'm not sure it's going to be a long-term thing. Though I share a lot more in common with him than my husband, there's a way in which he isn't available emotionally, either."

Heather shook her head with frustration, fighting back tears. "Maybe I should just live alone. I've thought about that, too, though it scares the hell out of me."

I reassured her and said, "Look, this may not be as difficult as you think. It seems to me you've got three clear choices here, right? Three possible paths you could take."

Her eyes brightened with the realization. "I suppose I do."

"And each of the choices has a consequence, right?"

"Yes . . ." I could sense her energy shifting as she started to get in touch with her own power again, her ability to take charge of her own life. As if thinking aloud, she outlined, in very realistic terms, the likely consequences of going back to her husband, staying with Mark, or moving away from both men and spending time alone.

"So, it's simple," I said. "Which consequence are you most willing to live with? Which will bring you the most growth?"

Heather shook her head with amazement. "God, it doesn't seem so difficult at all, when I look at it like that . . ."

A year later, Heather wrote to me in California. "I knew I needed to be alone, because I had never really done that," she said. "I needed to find myself without these men trying to define me and box me in. Thus began one of the most difficult, painful years I ever went through. But what a new richness it has brought me to within. Things are opening up for me in a way I couldn't even have dreamed of a year ago. I'm actually beginning to really like myself, and my relationship with spirit, the Source, grows deeper each day."

The Choosing process gets easier with practice. You get better at it. Try it out with small, relatively unimportant decisions, and then the method will work really beautifully when you have to make a major decision.

Eventually, you won't even have to think very much at all about what you're going to do in any given situation. You'll tune in to the energy of the moment, expand your vision, see all the options and consequences, and—bingo!—the obvious direction will show itself.

Honor your normal, human desires for success, love, pleasure, and material security—and the decisions that must be made around them—but don't let them rule you. Don't be so attached to them. Place the emphasis, instead, on seeking inner peace and happiness—the happiness that arises when you let go of outwardly striving and seeking and just relax into the *now* moment.

Let your desire for inner happiness be the driving desire in your life. Then all the others will fall into place. The outer things you need for your comfort and well-being will begin to come to you. You'll attract them.

## THE CREATIVE PROCESS

The creative power behind the universe—call it God, or the Source—re-creates itself most completely in the form of human beings like you and me, by endowing us with the power to create. Use your power wisely and responsibly, and you'll stay connected to the Source, to the light and energy of consciousness. You'll become an ever more clear and beautiful expression of the light.

To open to your true nature, you must *expand* your consciousness, but to make something happen in the world, you must *contract* to a certain degree, as you focus your energy and intention on the goal you wish to achieve. Finding the balance between expansion (being) and contraction (doing) is what the work of transformation is all about. The more established you are in your true nature, the more naturally you pull the energy in and focus it when you need to. Mastery of being leads to mastery of doing.

To get in the creative flow, you have to begin by stretching and flexing your creative muscles. Use your imagination. Play, explore, experiment with what it is you're trying to bring into being. Don't censor yourself, and don't be concerned with the final result. Just get into the process. Learn to trust the process.

True motivation comes from within. It's inbred, it's part of our true nature. People sometimes say to me, with a worried look on their faces, "But if I let go of my story, my fantasies, my ego, what will move me to *do* anything?"

I usually respond, "When you get your ego and your personal agendas out of the way, you become very clear, very present. The energy of the universe itself moves through you. You are inspired from within to act in new and creative ways. Goals take on a whole new meaning and purpose."

To create from a place of dissatisfaction and longing is to create in order to *get*. To create from a place of inner peace and fulfillment is to create in order to *give*. With the former, there's always the fear that your efforts will fail or won't be received in the way you want. With the latter, there's no fixation on outcome, no insistence on reward. Your creation is your gift to the world.

Understanding this will help you get clear about ambition. Ambition, when wielded by the ego, only reinforces the experience of arrogance and separation and leads inevitably to conflict and turmoil. You see this kind of aggressive personal ambition being played out in politics and business every day. But when ambition is used in the service of the heart, the highest good—as in the examples of people like Gandhi, Martin Luther King, Jr., and Mother Teresa—it produces results that benefit the well-being of everyone.

You're happiest when your own ambition has that selfless quality to it, that desire to really make a contribution to others. As Albert Schweitzer said, "I don't know what your destiny will be, but one thing I do know: the only ones among you who will be truly happy are those who have sought and found how to serve."

For true wholeness, *being* must be balanced with *doing*. Understand, then, the cycle of be-do-have. Too many people get it the wrong way round. They *do* what they think is necessary in order to *have* the things they believe will allow them to *be* happy.

The problem with do-have-be is that your happiness is then contingent upon *havingness*—and, as you know by now, this doesn't bring true inner peace. You start to get attached, and underneath the attachment is the fear of change, of losing what you've worked so hard to have. When you're attached to what happens, life is fraught with disappointment.

The intelligent way is to learn, first, simply to *be*—to be open to your true nature, the fullness of being. From here, you can then *do,* you can take action that springs from a deep sense of wholeness. Then you'll *have* the things in your life you want, but you won't be so attached to them. Your happiness will spring from beingness itself.

Discover the joy in being, do what you love, be grateful for what you have. To live this way is the surest path to both freedom and fulfillment.

Remember that you're a wave on the ocean of life. Be a wave. Make a big splash, if you want! Get out there and do something magnificent with your life or, at the very least, do what you have always wanted to do. But don't forget the ocean, the larger reality that is your true nature.

This is where the true power, the source of all creativity, love, and inspiration, is to be found.

## LOVE WILL GUIDE YOU

Love, you realize, is the highest and noblest expression of our true nature. Love is what got you here. Love is what sustains you. Love is what connects you with others. Love is what will, one day, allow you to make your transition out of this bodily existence easily and effortlessly, without fear.

When you live in balance with yourself and your environment, miracles unfold daily, and the greatest of them all is the miracle of love.

Hate is the ultimate disconnection from truth, from the great current of being that underlies all creation. Underneath hate is fear, the contracted energy of an ego—a "self"—that has forgotten its true nature and that has become (it thinks) a demigod, a power unto itself.

Jean Klein said it most eloquently: the ego is contraction, love is expansion. The ego is always seeking a cause, always trying to understand and control effects. Love is without cause, without conditions. The ego takes, grasps, consumes. Love just gives, endlessly.

The reality of love is a death-knell to the ego's illusions and fantasies. In the presence of authentic love, the ego doesn't stand a chance. When you're with someone who has no personal agenda, who just accepts and loves you unconditionally, your own "stuff" just sort of fades away. It's hard to remain contracted in the face of that kind of disarming openness.

This is why we need teachers and other awakened people to show us the way, to demonstrate that it is possible to be free. We have plenty of people who can model material success and achievement for us, who can show us how to find balance in the world of doing.

What we need more of are those who model enlightenment, real freedom, the mastery of being. Then, as each of us is touched by someone who is really conscious, who has seen through the illusion of "I" and "me" and whose heart is wide open, we are moved to look deep inside ourselves, to find the source of light within.

To get to the place where you feel free enough to connect with others in such an unconditionally loving way, you must feel safe. The only way to feel safe is to feel connected to a source of love bigger than yourself.

That source of love can't be another person, because another person's love can always be taken away. You've got to learn how to open to a universal source of love. To the divine love that has created you, and which sustains you in this body and this life.

Love is the most difficult lesson of all to learn but, like anything else, it gets easier with practice—and easier still as you open up to the core insight, as you expand your awareness and come into the realization of who you are beyond your body, mind, and conceptual ideas of self.

As you see through and let go of all the memories, beliefs, opinions, judgments, and concepts that you hold on to in your heart and mind, you'll start to experience a new freedom.

"Only a heart that has burned itself empty is capable of love," wrote Irina Tweedie, a Sufi teacher. The emptier you become of the past, of all illusory notions of "self," the more love you feel pouring through you.

You'll awaken to an inner peace and happiness that doesn't depend on circumstances, or on having to believe anything. Just to breathe deeply, to be in your body, your heart, to feel connected to the earth, to people, to your inner creative spirit, will be more than enough. It's all right here.

Your basic, underlying feeling will increasingly be one of gratitude for the gift of this life. This is when everything in your life will come into alignment and balance. This is when you'll know who you are, and what you're here to do. Then you'll no longer doubt yourself.

You'll relate differently to the problems in your life. Instead of worrying about them, you'll trust the deeper energy, the flow of love, the power of the present, to show you what to do. As it will, step by step. Indeed, love will begin to explode in all dimensions of your life—and, often, at the most unexpected moments.

The timeless power of love never fails. It will heal you and guide you every step of your journey here. Truly, as a great Western master of enlightenment, Jesus, taught us, perfect love casts out all fear. When you bring a clear and loving consciousness to your relationships, your work, and your creative endeavors, miracles happen.

If you're looking for a mission or purpose in life, try this: commit yourself fully to waking up and connecting with the love that is your true nature, so that you can then bring more love into the world.

You won't ever regret making such a commitment, and you'll start to experience an inner joy that will always be with you. What a gift to give yourself!

## EMBRACING CHANGE

Remember that change is the law of the universe. When change is inevitable, embrace it. You'll be glad you did. On the path of enlightenment, what you get is always better than what you let go of.

Be leery of trying to live by others' rules and precepts. William Blake said, "I must create a system of my own, or be enslaved by another man's." There's no "right" way to live your life, only the way that's right for you. If it's really right for you—at a heart and soul level—it will be right for the others in your life.

If you're young, you're blessed with a life of endless possibilities. You have so much before you, so many changes ahead. Welcome them, learn from them, and you'll become more completely the person you really are.

Older people too often become afraid of change. It shows in the narrowness of their thinking, the tightness in their bodies. It's never too late to reverse this trend, but it requires a major adjustment in attitude—an opening of the mind, a softening of the heart, compassion, and the courage to do something new or different.

If you're older and there's any trace in you of resentment of the young, then it's a sign you haven't been living fully. You're wasting your life in regret. Don't waste it any further. Start living *now*. Find out who you really are, the truth inside you that wants to come out.

Open your body, mind, and heart to the ever-new, ever-fresh energy of life. Remember, this is the key to always feeling young, no matter what your age. Go back and reread chapter 1. Learn what it takes to keep the life energy flowing through you.

As people age, they become more aware of the increasingly rapid passing of time. Time is movement, created by an "I," an ego that, all too often, clings to a past it's trying to forget and moves hesitantly toward a future it's not sure it wants.

Learn the difference between psychological time, the ego living in the past and future, and functional time, which is the natural evolution and expansion of creation. The past is what has given birth to the present. The future is the present expanding. Stand in the present, feel the expansion, and you'll realize that the future is *now*.

You'll realize, indeed, that you are never *not* in the present. Past and future exist only as ideas, concepts in the mind. Get caught up in your mind, especially in thoughts of "I" and "mine," and it will feel like you're somewhere else. But, in truth, the present, this moment now, is all that is real. Now, now, now.

You know you're free of the past when you look back at the memory of a particular relationship or event—especially one that was painful for you—and it's like another incarnation. The picture is there, but it has no feeling to it. There's no longer any emotional charge.

Time, according to the clock and calendar, is an arbitrary construct that plays an important role in human affairs. Use time, plan around it, but don't be attached to it. If you want to slow time down, stop counting it. Stop counting the hours, the days, the weeks, the months, the years. Then time won't be such a ruling influence in your life.

Live in the present, and you'll stop time altogether. If you really want to enjoy what you're doing, take your watch off. When you stop watching the clock, you're in the present. You're in the timeless space. When you pause to take notice, you'll be aware only of an endless flow of now-ness. See how simple it is?

On the journey of self-discovery you'll go through many births and transitions. With each letting go, with every new discovery, you'll emerge more fully as your real Self. Each time it will feel like a miracle.

You'll feel like you're dying and being reborn over and over again. At times this will be painful. The less you resist the process, the easier it will be. When you realize that change is necessary and you stop resisting it, change can occur much faster. Your transformation accelerates, and the birth you've been longing for—the liberation of your inner being, the unleashing of your true creative power—will soon happen.

When you finally awaken to your true nature, it will feel as though you fill every inch of your body. It's a very expanded feeling. You may find yourself saying, "Wow, I am really *me* for the very first time in my life!" Then you can just continue to grow as the person you truly are.

Eventually, as your realization of truth matures—and if you've focused on bringing it *into* your physical body, as opposed to just holding it at an intellectual level—you come to the place where your body feels very light and completely free of tension, so much so that it almost feels as if you don't have a body. You feel yourself as pure energy, pure spiritual presence, and your body has this wonderful flexibility, vitality, and strength to it.

When you, as consciousness, look inside yourself, into the

interior of your own being, not only are there no dark corners, no shadows in your psyche, but you also realize that you no longer have any substantial sense of self. You can't find a personal self anywhere! That's when you, as consciousness begin to comprehend just how free you are. You've completely seen through the story, the illusion of "I" and "me."

Before, you knew yourself as "John Smith" or "Mary Jones," and you just had glimpses of the pure consciousness, the clear, luminous awareness that is your true nature. Now you know yourself *as* that consciousness first, and "John Smith" or "Mary Jones" second. You realize that what you fundamentally are is awareness becoming aware of itself.

With this inner awakening, everything that is inessential in your outer life will begin to fall away. The forms will change, but the heart connection will be increasingly present. As you become more fully yourself, you'll let go of the relationships that don't support your being who you are, and you'll give energy to those that do. You won't waste time in jobs that you don't enjoy—or you'll find a way to enjoy them. You'll be sure to make space in your schedule for the creative work you love, for following your bliss.

What is false in our lives must, eventually, fall away, no matter how much we may kick and scream and desperately try to cling to it. The good news is that what is true remains and grows ever stronger. Let the false go; feed and nurture the true.

As the light and truth of being grow ever brighter and stronger in you, your constant feeling will be one of profound gratitude. What an extraordinary blessing it is, just to be here!

Remember to be thankful whenever anything good happens in your life, and even more good will come your way. That's the secret of abundance and prosperity, whether it's spiritual gifts such as love and kindness, or material gifts such as money, things, and opportunities in the world.

Be thankful, too, for your struggles and problems. See the blessing, the gift in them. Learn from them. They are there to show you where you may be out of balance, where you're not yet free. Like the "dark nights of the soul" I spoke of earlier, they are doorways to deeper levels of freedom.

## LIVE YOUR UNDERSTANDING

There's an end to the inner quest. It comes when your questions drop away and you realize you're no longer seeking anything. You've found yourself. Now you must live your understanding. Learning to do this is a lifelong process.

No matter how free you are, residues of your old self, your ego, will crop up periodically—of this you can be certain. Notice them, breathe through them, stay present, let them go. If there's learning to be had from these residual patterns, accept it.

Whenever you feel yourself getting out of balance, in conflict, look to your ego. Notice how you're thinking again in terms of "I," "me," and "mine." Release those three words, let them go each time they arise, and just *be*. Be open to something new. A miracle awaits you.

Enlightenment is a continuous dance between the impersonal and the personal. It's to live from your spirituality, from the clarity, unconditional love, and joy of your true nature, while fully honoring your humanity—your goals and desires, your relationship needs, your feelings, your creativity. This is the way of harmony—walking the inner path *in* the world. It is the surest way to reach balance, happiness, and success in your endeavors.

When you no longer need to give any names to the awesome energy that is at the heart of life but are able to just be totally open and present to it, then you will awaken to its full beauty, power, and wonder. This discovery will blow your mind, open your heart, and transform your life.

Never doubt the truth you've discovered. When doubts do come up, face them. Breathe into them. See through them. Remember, you are bigger than them. They are not who you are. Take heart, too, in the fact that even the most enlightened individuals are still human and can experience doubt—albeit fleetingly—from time to time.

The proof that you're on the right path is that living starts to become more effortless. It has a wonderful feel of balance and flow to it. It's not that you won't have to exert "effort" at times, but it won't be a struggle. You won't experience internal conflict. You'll take care of business, of your responsibilities and obligations, in a wise, compassionate, and decisive way.

Pass on the gift that has been given you. Share the message of this book with others. This is the way to ensure you'll always have it yourself. When others seem open to it (and only when!), gently remind them of what is real. Remind them that they are not their beliefs, their circumstances, their "story." Remind them of who they really are—that their true nature is consciousness, awareness, and that they are always free. That happiness is what is there when they get themselves out of the way.

When you speak to others from this new consciousness, you'll find a strength and power to your words that wasn't there before. When you are not yet fully awake, you tend to talk in terms of theories, beliefs, and concepts. You speculate about what you hope or imagine might be true. But when you really wake up, the theories drop away and you speak just from your experience.

Pause often to breathe, be still, and tune in to the deeper energy that is always here. Let your awareness expand. See the beauty. Feel it. Feel the whole of creation vibrating within and around you. Feel the power of the present. Get really centered in your body, pull the energy in, let it flow out to everyone and everything you touch. Be the magnificent person you are.

When love is shared, it grows and increases, and your heart fills with joy. When it's held on to, it contracts and diminishes, and your heart becomes empty and lonely. Go back through this book as often as you need or wish, until the core insight, the tools, and the information I've shared become real for you. It's the core insight that will free you from the negative grip of your past, your story, and the illusion of fear. It's the core insight that will open your heart and unlock the door to the inexhaustible well of love and wisdom within you.

It's so, so simple, really, though it takes a long time for most of us to actually "get" it. But when you see that the story inside your head is not real, that it's a myth of your own creation, you stop giving energy to it and it starts to fall away.

With the dropping away of the story, of the past, your head becomes very clear, astonishingly so. You're able to see everything without distortion. In the pristine clarity that is your natural awareness you hear the voice of wisdom—the voice that *wants* to come through you—and it speaks directly from your heart, in the present, in the form of insight, intuition, intelligence, and love.

You no longer have to worry about what to do when you're facing a problem or a decision. Consciousness itself is the transformative agent. When you shine the light of consciousness, of awareness, on any problem, the layers of confusion and perplexity surrounding the situation soon start to dissolve, to peel away. The problem reveals its solution to you. It draws the creativity, the ingenuity, the needed words or actions right out of you.

It all happens by itself, spontaneously, and you're just the instrument through which it happens. What a blast, what a joy, living becomes when you have this kind of trust and inner freedom. How totally satisfying, nurturing, and fulfilling it is. And what freshness, what richness it brings into your life!

Our planet yearns for balance, for healing, for wholeness. That's why spiritual awakening, or enlightenment, is so important. It's the *only* way to get free of fear and to ensure that we use our material and technological progress wisely, in a way that benefits all of humanity. Otherwise, we just end up creating an even wider gulf between the privileged few and the struggling many, with all the negative consequences that such unconsciousness brings, not just socially and politically but environmentally, as well.

As your own life starts to come together, inwardly and outwardly, you'll be inspired to show others how to travel the way of harmony. You'll want to speak your truth and share your love, your happiness, your good fortune with others.

Do it! The world is waiting for it.

# Index